INVESTING
FOR
RETIREMENT

INVESTING
FOR
RETIREMENT

A Successful Recipe for the
Buying and Selling of
Stocks for IRA's and
Other Retirement Plans

By
Jacob Katz

Copyright © 1992 by Jacob Katz

Library of Congress Catalog Card Number 92-90580

ISBN 0-9603986-4-3

PTI Publishing
Pittsburgh, Pennsylvania

First Printing, September 1992

Cover Design by Christopher Foster

Printed in the U.S.A by
BookMasters, Inc.
1444 U.S. Route 42 RD #11
Mansfield, OH 44903

DEDICATION

I wrote this book for my dear family and friends in the hope they can use some of the stock market ideas, especially as these ideas apply to their retirement assets. I hope this book holds true to a quote of Henry Wadsworth Longfellow, "Give what you have. To someone, it may be better than you dare think."

ACKNOWLEDGEMENTS

It was in 1979 when I wrote a practical book on how to understand and cope with the Electrostatic Precipitator, a piece of equipment which has given major problems to industrial personnel for well over 70 years. The positive response to the precipitator book from many readers actually gave me the encouragement to undertake another "How-To" book. I would like to thank all of those persons for sharing their helpful comments to me.

No book can be brought to a conclusion without the help of many people. My son, Owen, gave me some in-depth financial comments which were extremely valuable. Other family members were supportive and provided a number of good thoughts on the text. Nancy Lynches and Jim Mendrzycki provided helpful guidance in the technical aspects of market procedures. Art Candido reviewed the draft and offered valid comments and encouragement, as did Dr. Larry Seidman.

Special thanks goes to Dr. Karen Hjelmervik, who not only helped shape up my first book, but again provided the expertise and guidance to produce some sense from my writing in this endeavor. I also appreciate the typing and cooperation of Joseph Czolnik in producing the drafts and finished copy.

My sincere thanks to all!

CONTENTS

PREFACE

Is another book needed on investments in the stock market? Yes, it is, and that's because I believe it's time to encourage a new generation of investors to join the stock market, and also to win back disillusioned ones who have quit.

This book is a contribution to that effort. I wrote it primarily for the person who has a tax-sheltered investment portfolio such as an Individual Retirement Account (IRA), Keogh, or any other self-directed retirement plan. But it's also intended for people between the ages of 25 – 40 who should begin today planning for their retirements.

And now is a good time to begin, it is extremely easy to set up a self-directed retirement plan. Practically all brokerage houses, mutual funds, and banks have a prototype plan approved by the Internal Revenue Service. The tax-deferment status of these plans makes the stock program I am recommending a viable one for investment success.

What kind of expert am I to be passing on advice about retirement investments? Actually, the best kind. I'm a self-employed consulting engineer – I've been one for nearly 30 years – and I've had to invest carefully over the years in order to reach my goal of a secure retirement. And I have achieved it. I've developed a technique that has worked for me, and now I want to pass on what I've learned to those who are as concerned about their investments as I have been about mine.

Why haven't I trusted a firm to handle my investments? First, I've learned that there is no person or firm that can really predict what's going to happen in the market, and by following a well planned program, I can do as well as most experts. Second, I like the excitement of the market, and I want to participate. But most importantly, I believe the growth and protection of my retirement assets are too important to be left completely to others.

1

And what are my ideas? There's no magic here. In fact, I have based my program on common sense and self-discipline, not on fancy predictions based on many complicated variables. I stress a few principles that even busy people can tailor to their needs. These principles include investing as early in life as you can, choosing companies you can afford the time to follow, staying safe and conservative, and avoiding greed and anxiety.

I don't promise riches, but I do believe that this program is more likely to make your retirement investment grow at a satisfactory above-market rate. Finally, I'd like you to join me in successfully directing your own investments because I've always said a person can't have too many friends.

J. Katz 1992

CHAPTER 1: INTRODUCTION

Millions of persons in this country have a right to be concerned about their retirement years. Many companies are shifting the burden of decisions for pension investments to the individual employee. The long-term future of Social Security is somewhat suspect, and even if it exists in the form we know it, Social Security may not provide much more than minimal subsistence. The self-employed business person or professional has to make retirement assets grow at a satisfactory rate.

The stock market happens to be the place that offers one of the best ways to achieve financial success for retirement purposes, but unfortunately, very few persons reap its benefits on an individual basis. This situation comes about for many reasons, but primarily, it is a lack of knowing how to cope with uncertainty. However, I have found over many years that it is the very uncertainty of the market that provides the greatest chance for the average investor to do well. If you want to achieve above average results by self-directing your own investment decisions, the ideas in this book will help you. These ideas and concepts run contrary to some established practices, but they have worked for me, and I believe they will work well for you.

The last thing you need from me is more confusion from a comprehensive "menu" of investment tools. I am not going to discuss options, margin, short-selling, and other specialized techniques. There are relatively simple investment tools that can provide you success in the stock market. I believe that the simpler the steps you take, the greater your chance for building confidence and success in your investments.

I have always been fascinated by the ability of the stock market to fool its participants. And even though I will offer a number of steps that have proven successful for me, I do not want you to think this presentation will be a type of foolproof approach. That would be nice, but it is not realistic where

3

so many different factors exist at the same time. In fact, it would be quite difficult to find any group of simple ideas and concepts that always work well in the stock market. On the other hand, some ideas appear to have more merit than others, and it will be this valuable group of ideas that I will describe. You might find it useful to read this book more than once to get all of its real value. The subject of one's retirement is too important and the implications too great for just a cursory treatment.

You are not going to receive techniques in this book that can double or triple your money in a short period. Sure, such gains can occur, but I down play "speculation," while I stress methodical investment techniques. I believe that if your objective is to play in the sun in later years, it is better to be known as the tortoise who won the race.

But you'll still see action. In the long-term approach to stock investing described in detail in Chapter 5, there will be many opportunities for you to experience the excitement of the market. Every stock purchase will be earmarked for a potential sell at a reasonable profit. Therefore, the activity of trading itself should whet your appetite for action.

However, investing for one's future retirement must never be placed in the class of a gamble. Trading stocks in a tax-deferred pension plan should be considered a strategy for investment safety. What better way to assure a significant profit than to take it when that profit is present. And since you defer any tax on the gain of that sale, you have materially increased the cash assets that now becomes available for your next transaction.

The term "trading" often suggests a rapid in-and-out set of stock transactions to achieve relatively small profits on those trades. This type of trading is not considered a conservative technique, and its use would not be prudent for pension plans. In fact, the small to medium pension investor would probably find it difficult to produce good results with excessive trading because of the costs of brokerage commissions as well as the time required to implement that type of program. The success of the buy and sell concepts of this book is predicated on achieving a significant percentage gain from the transaction, and the time frame between trades can range from as little as a week to as long as a couple of years for a specific stock.

My recommended investment technique means thinking of your program in terms of income enhancement rather than just as a gain in the price appreciation of stock. In other words, you want to achieve income growth above the rate of income that will be needed for your eventual retirement years. This usually means you must set your goal for beating the percentage return from fixed income investments such as certificates of deposit or bonds.

The main reason I have developed a technique utilizing stock investment for the pension plan is that stocks work well during practically all the changes of the economy. You have to be vigilant against the complacency that could occur in an easy money environment that may only last for a relatively short period of time.

For example, the purchase of certificates of deposit when the interest rates are high, such as occurred in 1981, can provide a very satisfactory return on your investment. But what happens when those certificates mature during an environment of low interest rates?

It makes sense for you to develop the confidence in stock investment. You can acquire this confidence in the stock market by using a few simple principles to achieve success. This confidence will take time, of course, but your knowledge will minimize the uncertainty for making your pension portfolio grow in value.

REQUIREMENTS FOR SUCCESS

You will not need a technical background or require a business school education to understand this book. Moreover, you will find there are other personal qualities more likely to lead to your success in the stock market than a high degree of intelligence.

For example, your ability to be patient when investment decisions are not going right and not be swayed by emotions, and to be able to invest contrary to most other people are qualities that matter more than intelligence. The principles presented in this book help to develop these qualities if you do not already possess them.

SOURCES OF INFORMATION

My years of experience in the stock market have been made up of failures and successes. A poor decision is the best teacher. By stating some key investment concepts simply, I hope to minimize those same mistakes in your stock program.

Of course, I have also spent many thousands of hours in reading books, magazines, newspapers, advisory letters, and listening to radio and television information over the years. It is difficult to remember just who and where all of the information came from, but in the last chapter of the book, I've described sources that helped me the most.

There is both a disadvantage and advantage in absorbing the many ideas of investing in the stock market. It is easy to become indecisive when a number of recommendations appear to conflict with one another. Nevertheless, it is wise to keep gathering information on a continuous basis because the market keeps going through ups and downs, and you should stay alert to these variations. Think of the following chapters as aids to developing your confidence.

BACKGROUND EXPERIENCES OF AUTHOR

I made all the classic mistakes of most uninformed investors. For example, I missed an opportune time for investing in stocks in the post-World War II years. This missed opportunity was not for lack of advice. A college classmate told me to buy Reynolds Metal in 1948. I calmly replied I was not interested in the stock market. Of course I was not interested – I knew nothing about it. And the G.I. Bill certainly did not provide any extra money for stock purchases. In retrospect, stocks of most well-known companies that were purchased between 1948 and 1960 would have been a sound investment.

Later, when I was interested in about 1955, the hot tips I was given reduced my small savings to practically zero, but I did own some shares in a copper mine in Peru and a columbium mine in Canada. That experience soured me on the stock market for a period, but eventually I got involved in a stock purchase plan with my employer, US Steel Corp. After leaving US Steel, I felt that the automobile industry was booming, so I promptly converted my US Steel shares into the stock of General Motors in 1963. I caught the auto industry at a peak, and subsequently lost about 50% of my portfolio value. Those were not the only mistakes I made in the next ten years, but you get the picture – I was your average investor getting whipsawed without knowing why.

The period of 1971 – 1974 produced the last straw. After the start of a corporate pension plan in 1971, I saw my fully invested portfolio drastically fall in value during the 1974 market drop. It was during 1974 that I began a serious attempt to understand the market and to develop investing methods that would minimize the mistakes of my past.

ELEMENTS OF THE RECOMMENDED TECHNIQUE

It is only in retrospect that the reasons for failure sometimes become a little clearer. On a day-to-day basis I am as confused as the next person as to why the prices of stocks reverse direction. The reasons are not generally understood. Once you recognize that the price movements in the stock market are difficult to predict, use that knowledge to your advantage.

In most of my poor investment decisions, my underlying mistake was to be highly invested in stocks without having sufficient cash in reserve. I then had to either wait out a lengthy time period during a decline in the market or take the loss and sell in order to generate cash. So I learned that the direction of the stock market can turn rapidly and balancing a stock portfolio with a cash reserve is needed for success.

Another lesson I learned was that I should have determined how the stock price compared to its high for the year before I decided to make the purchase. For example, I was naive and purchased the stock of General Motors in 1963 near its high price for the year. The down-side risk is always greatest at this point in the pattern of stock prices, especially for the large, mature companies.

Even then, I made another classic mistake in the 1971 – 1974 period that taught me yet another important lesson – **Do Not Be Greedy!** I started to buy stock in 1971 as prices were rising and continued to purchase stocks without regard to the appreciation already achieved in my portfolio. When the market drop occurred, I felt that it was only a temporary set-back and I wanted to regain those profits seen earlier. Needless to say, I didn't raise cash, and the value of the portfolio retreated well below the original purchase levels. You can see how easy it was for me to let my emotions control my actions in the stock market.

It is discouraging to watch a portfolio rise and fall in value without reaping anything out of that cycle. Certainly that experience taught me that cycles of the stock price variations should be used advantageously. I began to study the historical price movements of stocks dating back for a number of years. This information confirmed for me that the high and low stock prices of many large companies formed patterns that almost repeated themselves each year or so. The seed of an investing method was planted.

I learned also that success from purchasing stocks based on hot tips does not often occur. At least, it is a chancy way to invest. The basis of my recommended technique, described in Chapter 5, is to specialize in a small group of stocks you are comfortable with, and whose price movements you can follow over a period of years. This method of investing down-plays the emotional factor of jumping from company to company, based on random recommendations while hoping to achieve a big score. One key word is patience, and another is self-discipline.

A successful investment method for stocks must, at a minimum, be comprised of several key elements:

1. Always maintain a significant cash reserve relative to the total value of the stocks in your portfolio.

2. Learn the yearly price variations of the stocks you are following and buy at their low levels, rather than at the higher end of the price range.

3. Learn to take profits at reasonable points of stock appreciation. Do not be greedy by reaching for maximum returns on your investments.

4. Minimize reacting to the continuous bombardment of recommendations and hot tips from others. Develop a satisfactory investment technique, get confident with it, and discipline yourself to make it successful.

There is no magical formula for success in the stock market. These guidelines should be considered basic for any investor, but their application year in and year out becomes a challenge. But I will weave them into a reasonable program in which you can self-direct a retirement portfolio of stocks with confidence. The one main concept that is the cornerstone of this technique is how much cash you are holding at any given time. This cash amount is basically the driving force in how active you become in your trading of stocks; when cash is low, you are looking to sell, and when cash is high, you are looking to buy. This is a simple, yet effective concept that you will learn brings some discipline to your program.

There will be a countless number of variables that affect the stock price of any company over time. The astute investor will have to take the above guidelines along with some bits of knowledge contained in this book and refine a method that can last a lifetime.

CHAPTER 2: PHILOSOPHY OF THE STOCK MARKET

How much information is needed for a person to become good at any activity? Some activities actually become difficult to comprehend with too much diverse information. Read too many instructional books on golf, and you can become a basket case. Reading too much about the stock market can do the same thing.

Part of the learning process in the field of stock investing is to recognize this confusion. When three respected advisors can take the same basic information and form three different opinions as to where the market is heading, you know that no one has the answer.

I have developed a method of investing that does not require a lot of advice to help keep you on a successful path. But confidence in any activity is primarily comprised of knowing the territory, and for that reason, in this chapter, I have provided some necessary background information. You should skim the information you already know. If you are new to the world of the stock market, I believe you will find it a simple primer of investment philosophy and what tends to occur in the transactions of the market.

HOW THE MARKET WORKS

If you are going to participate in the stock market, you must have a fundamental knowledge of how it functions. The stock market is an auction in which someone owns a product and decides to trade it for cash to someone who believes the product is worth owning. This activity takes place at some exchange location, and possibly two or three middle persons handle the transaction between the buyer and the seller.

The stock market transaction represents the buying and selling of a small part of an established company, normally characterized by the term common shares. When a company is publicly traded, it will have a great number of common shares outstanding or available for sale. These shares represent a portion of the perceived existing worth of the company at a specific point in time. Usually only a very small percentage of each company's outstanding shares (capitalization) are traded during any given day, but the price agreed upon also affects the total market value of all the outstanding shares.

Some companies may lose 2% to 3% of their total market value in one day, yet there may be no basic change in their business outlook or assets. It may only be a perception of groups of investors that at a given point in time, a company is worth much less that it was maybe a few days earlier. But do not forget – for every seller there is a buyer who has an opposite opinion of the company.

In most of these transactions, neither the seller nor the buyer really has any solid idea of the true underlying structure of these companies. There is nothing basically wrong with that situation. After all, automobiles are bought and sold every day without people knowing all the details of the equipment under the hood.

An interesting factor is how the movement of the stock price from all this buy and sell action affects the market worth of a company. Let's take a well-known company, Goodyear Tire and Rubber Co., and show its market action for the month of December 1980. There were 1,842,800 shares of Goodyear stock traded during that month at a price that ranged from $15 – $16\frac{3}{4}$ per share. This monthly trading represented about $2\frac{1}{2}$% of all the 71,761,000 outstanding shares of Goodyear. Sometime during December, the market value of Goodyear then varied by approximately 126 million dollars between the two extreme points of its stock swing. That would coincide with a drop of 10.4% in market value, if you consider the price decline from the $16\frac{3}{4}$ to the $15 level. Was Goodyear worth only about 90% of a previous value set sometime during the thirty day period? Consider that $97\frac{1}{2}$% of all the outstanding shares did not contribute to that decision. You can observe this same type of price movement for the stock of most companies that are listed on the stock exchanges.

What should this all mean to you on a day-to-day basis? It should not signify much more than that the marketplace is a viable, pulsating activity, where often sizeable changes occur in the perceived worth of a specific company. The name of the game is perception, and how you perceive a company's future must be different from someone else's if the transaction is to occur in the first place.

I will later discuss some of the common sense ways you can sharpen your perception of the potential value of the stock of a company. Even a so-called conservative company like Goodyear can be perceived to be glamorous at some point in time.

Common shares represent a part ownership of a company and the transaction of these shares is primarily the transfer of dollars for a commodity. That commodity could include buildings, machinery, land, trees, oil, coal, gold, copper, or a hundred other types of assets of measurable value. In other words, a stock transaction should not be considered only a transfer of a paper certificate.

I have often heard comments in past years that it is much better to own a piece of land or other tangible commodity than to hold stocks during an inflationary period. It appears to me that owning a part of a forest company or an oil company can also be considered a good hedge against an upward inflationary environment.

At the same time, dividends will produce an income during the holding period of a stock portfolio. Add to this situation the liquidity of the stock market, or the ability to readily trade your asset for cash on the open market, and I believe that you have the potential for as much safety of your funds as one can hope for when compared to many other types of investments.

THE EXCHANGES

Most persons are acquainted with the three major exchanges that handle the transactions of stocks. The New York Stock Exchange (NYSE) is headquartered on Wall Street and is sometimes called the Big Board. The larger companies, including the thirty companies that comprise the Dow Jones Industrial Average, will generally be found on this exchange. The American Stock Exchange (ASE), sometimes referred to as AMEX, is also located in New York City. In addition, there are smaller regional exchanges throughout the country. The Over-the-Counter (O-T-C) stocks are primarily traded through a group of offices forming the National Association of Security Dealers (NASD).

There are guidelines, government rules, audits, and any number of policing actions to help assure a high degree of reliability and honesty in the financial marketplace. Is it perfectly reliable without any foul-ups? No, there is always the human element that might surface with a transaction.

The overall procedure, starting with the initiation of a stock transaction to its final completion, is accomplished on trust. Thousands of dollars go through this process, primarily based on a person's word, and very few mistakes or problems develop compared to the large number of transactions that occur each market day. The whole stock market system would breakdown if a lack of confidence began to occur between the participants. The stakes are high and these high confidence levels have to be maintained.

WHAT IS A SAFE INVESTMENT?

It's nice to talk about complete safety, but that term is elusive when it refers to investments. The safety of investments is based on a multitude of factors and it is more prudent to think of the relative safety of one investment against another. One main element of safety in any investment program is to have your funds grow faster than the rate of inflation.

The above statement refers to the safety of growth and this primarily relates to your overall investment. In other words, it is perfectly satisfactory to lose 10% of an investment and achieve a 25% growth in the remaining 90% of your funds for a net return of $12^1/_2\%$. But if you lost 10% of your investment and made only a 15% return on the remaining 90%, the net gain of your portfolio for the year would be $3^1/_2\%$. That would be unsatisfactory since it would be below the normal rate of inflation of recent years.

I believe a key to the safety of growth of any program is to minimize the complete loss of any existing portion of your investments. So the quality of the investment is of primary importance. Fortunately, the investment in stocks can be selected from financially secure companies to help minimize the chance for loss.

The safety of an investment program can also be affected by its diversification. The definition of diversification can take many turns when it comes to an investment. The most common viewpoint, especially in recent times, is to consider the allocation of funds into several different types of investments.

For example, in the allocation technique, you could split your funds into four parts and invest 25% into each of the areas of real estate, bonds, stocks, and cash. This is a hedge technique where you are hoping that if the bond market retreats in price, the real estate market would tend to appreciate, thus counteracting the effect of the depreciation in the bond price on the value of your portfolio. This technique of diversification, while it looks good at first, has the danger of gains and losses nearly cancelling each other out.

There are variations of the allocation technique where you can apply a timing factor for shifting funds from one investment to another. Some investors allot part of their funds to the purchase of gold, coins, diamonds, art, stamps, and even comic books. All of these areas require a high degree of knowledge and even then, these investments are subjected to random swings of high profits or losses. One universal rule of investing is that the higher the risk, the greater potential for gains, and conversely, the greater potential for losses. That is the main reason why I settled on a simple stock technique with less risk, but of course, with the expectation of only reasonable returns.

Though I am not going to stress the buying of bonds or gold, that does not mean successful programs cannot be achieved from a variety of investments. If you are comfortable with owning some gold or art, then do so by all means. The purpose of this book is not to discourage other areas of investment but rather to help supply the knowledge and confidence for you to invest in stocks.

My belief in the safety of investments relates to a portfolio of stocks from a broad base of quality companies that is coupled with the maintenance of optimum cash reserves. This mix of assets minimizes the possibility of getting whipsawed with several different types of investments. At the same time, it allows for liquidity in both a rising and falling economy. Based on what I have observed over the years, cash can be as good a commodity to have at times as anything else I know.

IS THERE A MARKET CONSPIRACY?

There might be a natural tendency to view the financial community, the so-called moguls of Wall Street, and others, as acting in some puppet-pulling conspiracy that controls the stock market. Of course, there have been occasions in past years, as well as in recent times, where individuals or groups have made excessive profits from insider trading or scams of various types. As long as there are humans involved, there will be the possibility of unethical dealings.

Fortunately, I believe the percentage of stock manipulation against total transactions is minuscule for practically all the established companies on the stock exchanges. The stock market is under the observation of thousands of professional investment managers and advisors and is exceedingly difficult to manipulate. I would like to enlarge on some of my thoughts in this regard because if you do not develop confidence in the marketplace, it might be quite easy for you to forsake stocks at your first losses.

One area of discussion concerns the role of the specialists. I do not see too much wrong with their activity. In fact, knowledge of how the specialists perform actually adds to the success of the stock trading technique discussed in Chapter 5. Let me describe the job of the specialist as I understand, it and I believe you will agree that what they do appears to have more advantages for the small investor than disadvantages.

The specialists are usually investment or banking concerns who have been assigned one or more of the companies that are listed on the NYSE and ASE. These specialists must have sufficient cash reserves which are utilized to conduct orderly trading in the stocks for which they are responsible. They act as the intermediary between the buyer and seller of stocks. These specialists basically determine the degree of the rise and fall of the prices of the stocks they handle, dependent on both the open orders that are recorded in their future transaction book and the instantaneous pressures of market orders.

When many more sellers exist for a particular stock than buyers, prices will tend to fall rapidly, and the specialist is obligated to use the firm's funds to purchase enough of the excess shares on the market to help stabilize the stock price at a new level. It is also reasonable to expect the specialists to sell off part of their accumulated stock portfolio to the new buyers that enter a rising market. Persons still holding stock in a rising market are not prone to sell immediately, so the inventory held by the specialist becomes a necessary ballast to help keep stock prices from rising in large steps. This activity in recent years is primarily directed toward the retail end of the market where relatively small blocks of stock are transferred between the participants.

The specialist system does appear to help prevent one-day drops or rises in stock prices from becoming excessive. In other words, it does what it was meant to do, even though the average person outside the exchange, including myself, can only marvel at the procedures. There appeared to be a break-down in the specialist system somewhat during the October 1987 market free fall. Some efforts to minimize the potential for that type of market action have already been put in place, but it is difficult to know exactly what happened during that one-day 500 plus point drop in the Dow Jones Average.

The specialist earns money in several ways. First, a small percentage of the cost of each trade transaction is retained. Second, the stocks purchased and placed in inventory are later sold for some profit as the market recovers. And the third method is to short their specific stocks for later purchase, a practice some question.

To short a stock is a technique where an investor sells a stock without actually owning it and then later buys the stock, hopefully, at a lower price. The stock that is later purchased is then used to replenish the original stock that was borrowed for the short-sale. The money difference between the original sale and the later purchase of the stock, minus some costs, becomes the net profit of the transaction. For purposes of this book, the simplified short sale procedure described above is for information, and is not recommended for the persons with retirement funds to invest in established plans.

Nevertheless, the short sale is employed by certain investors, including the specialist. Critics of the specialists would then state that the knowledge of the open orders in their book places the specialist at an advantage in applying the short-sale. However, I still cannot believe the specialist alone can turn a market around against the great multitude of factors that affect the direction of stock prices. The specialists make money employing knowledge gleaned from market signs, that's true, but all sorts of persons read signs of supply and demand. The fact that officials of the securities commission approve of this practice and monitor it for abuses is satisfactory for me.

Also, if the specialists had all the power attributed to them, why do many of their stocks languish for months in a narrow price range and at low volume? I believe outside forces tend to get the stock price moving in some direction and the specialist primarily provides some control over its rate of change. Consider the thousands of independent people from all over the country who make their living advising and predicting the directions of stock prices. I was never aware of any conspiracy talk concerning specialists from this knowledgeable group of market watchers.

If the specialists play a pivotal part in the daily transactions of stocks, and they are in a position to be knowledgeable about the stocks they handle, and they are in business to earn good profits, I want to be on their side.

The specialists must buy stocks in a declining market and sell these stocks back in a rising market. If the specialists have to accumulate stocks in a down market as part of their arrangement, it makes sense that the last groups of stocks bought will then be sold at a higher price on the way up, and so forth.

An investment technique that follows the buying and selling patterns of the specialists is sure to have a solid foundation to be able to achieve reasonable success over the years and that makes sense to me.

ECONOMIC EFFECT ON THE MARKET

The underlying strengths and weaknesses observed in the stock market are basically related to the domestic and world economies and the growth or decline of various business activity. Certainly, there are other factors, but when business is booming, the chance that many stocks will also be booming is pretty good.

An underlying optimism about the ability of our country to overcome economic problems must be ever–present in your thinking. That does not mean you should be happy with everything that happens in the economy. But unless you as an investor can cope with severe economic problems that crop up every few years without feeling your world is falling apart, you will have some difficulty investing successfully in the stock market.

You should have some confidence in our ability to overcome adversary and maintain our position as the largest and strongest consuming market in the world. Evidently, other countries have that confidence or foreign money would not pour into the USA every time there is some fear generated in the world. And the increase of foreign investment in our country should not be construed as the end of the world for us. But is does indicate economic conditions have changed in recent years. The point I am stressing is that you should be aware of changing times.

The period extending from the conclusion of World War II to about 1962, produced a steady upward growth in the stock market as our country boomed in the economic good times. If you owned stocks in any of the basic industries such as autos, construction, housing, steel, machinery, and so forth, it was difficult not to prosper during this period as the strong demand for goods and services were being met. The USA was also helping to rebuild other countries in the world.

Even though some temporary economic set-backs did occur, a strategy to buy and hold stocks in many of the well-known companies during this period of time proved pretty successful. When the labor market pushed for a piece of the economic pie, business leaders could satisfy those demands with little problem. After all, prices could be raised because of the demand for these products, and everyone was on a merry cycle.

This Buy and Hold strategy of stocks did not work too well in the decade of the 70's. Competition from other countries began to be felt. Oil prices rose drastically. Environmental laws produced uncertainty. Productivity decreased as some of the practices that existed in earlier years came back to haunt many companies when times became tougher.

As a country matures, everything becomes more complex in that every rise and fall in supply and demand affects economic activity. Remember that each mature company can also be drastically affected by relatively minor changes in the demand for its products. While maturity has its advantages, it must also be continually monitored for its health. That is why the Buy and Hold strategy of previous years appear to be less prudent today as an investment approach for most of the well established stocks.

In the near term, the stock market should reflect the painful periods of correcting the areas of economic difficulty. The bailout of the savings and loan industry can stagger the imagination. As the country gets its priorities straightened out, I foresee an extended period of good times in the stock market. Furthermore, if you are optimistic about our country's future, then the stock market is basically an optimistic area for investing.

STOCK MARKET PSYCHOLOGY

I would be remiss not to discuss the psychological aspects of the stock market. This will not be a complicated coverage because I have a tough time even spelling psychological. I do know there are times that the stock market overreacts to certain news to a much greater degree than warranted. At other times, certain stocks climb rapidly in price or trend downward over periods of time because of the perception of investors based on various financial information. These periods are part of the game, and your mind has to be conditioned to the quirks of crowd psychology and how this factor effects the stock market.

Probably of prime psychological concern should be your own personality regarding the movement of stock prices. You may never know exactly how you will react until you start investing in the market, but there are a couple of warning signs. If you ever gamble at cards or at the race track, and your stomach churns at the bet you lost, maybe the stock market is not for you. Nobody expects a person to smile while losing, but your personality must be able to accept some loss gracefully. Even though the investing technique I will be discussing later should minimize the major valuation set-backs in your portfolio, stock prices will always gyrate along the way. At the same time, you should learn to accept appreciable stock gains without the feeling that you want to blow a bugle while standing on your roof at midnight.

The movement of stock prices are continually publicized on a daily basis, and these short-term price changes often resemble a roller-coaster ride. I believe that after you complete this book, you will feel comfortable with swings in stock prices. In fact, you should even begin to look forward to the downward swings as buying opportunities. At those times, I am suggesting that you begin to feel like the little boy thrashing through a large pile of manure while saying that there must be a pony in there someplace. But, if after you start investing in stocks and you still find it difficult to stay relatively calm and confident with minor price gyrations, then the market may not be for you.

Once your own personality and the price variations of stocks become compatible, you will have to learn how to cope with the psychological pushes and pulls of the overall market. This is an area of discipline that can be learned, and I will discuss a number of factors that may help you.

I mentioned earlier that the buying and selling pressures in the stock market primarily determine the direction and degree of a stock trend. This trend, once started, often continues to move too far in the direction taken – much like the swing of a pendulum past its center point.

At a given point in time, a whole industry may be stated to have little earnings potential because of certain economic projections. This information could have been distributed in a financial publication or a report from a brokerage house. Consequently, a sell-off of stocks in this industry group begins which tends to pick up momentum. It is conceivable for 10% to 15% of the market value of those companies to get wiped out before their stock prices stabilize at a new level. In other words, the psychology of the crowd produced an avalanche of sellers and few buyers. If you want to later buy a stock in that out-of-favor industry, a tremendous psychological battle usually takes place. You might have to overcome the advice of brokers, analysts, and various publications for you to be able to make that purchase. It becomes difficult to buck a trend. I often tell myself that someone else bought those stocks on the way down and at the stabilized zone, and might they not be insiders or specialists, or just plain bargain-hunters? And what is possibly wrong with that group of buyers? Heavy gloom in the stock market should make you somewhat optimistic towards purchasing stock.

Another psychological pressure works to make you want to buy a certain stock after it has appreciably risen from being well-publicized and recommended by advisors and brokerage houses. The fact that the stock is being touted as a good buy and it is rising in price is a reasonably good sign. Some of my early reading suggested that this is actually a time to buy. From a psychological standpoint, it may be easier to buy a stock when it is showing price gains each day. Unfortunately, this knowledge is usually observed or found out when the stock has already moved appreciably from its low price level of the preceding year.

It pays to understand who the sellers of the stocks were in the rising market. Were the sellers made up of insiders, specialists, or persons who just simply bought the stocks at a low price and were selling off for a good gain? The selling group in a rising market certainly would not turn around and buy again at a higher price. So if I bought their stocks, who would be around to buy from me. Stock market literature might refer sometimes to a"greater fool theory," which means every buyer hopes there is somebody out there who will eventually buy his asset at a still higher price. High levels of stock market optimism should make you somewhat wary about adding to your stocks.

Whether buying stocks will pay off for you when their prices are at a low point of a range or after their prices have already advanced in a rising market, can only be known after the fact of the transaction. The basis of this book keeps going back to the low point case as being more prudent for the investing of pension money, if it is accomplished in a disciplined manner.

One would believe that in recent years, with the advent of professional managers of pension funds and mutual funds, that the market would be exempt from the affects of major psychological moves. However, emotions can run as far and as deep with persons running the large investment firms as they can with the individual investor. It is easy to understand that as the number of funds grows and they all have to compete for the investing dollar, the performance of each fund becomes important for its growth. This situation has led to frequent turnovers of stock positions in these funds. This factor can actually work in favor of the small investor since large funds tend to rotate their investment activity among the same groups of the larger capitalized companies.

The above concepts point toward a method of investing that basically says you should buck the trend and become a contrarian in your actions. A formula for success cannot be that simple, but there are valid assumptions behind the contrarian concept. For example, if heavy market selling has substantially driven stock prices downward, then investing in those stocks that have fallen the most in price will generally allow for the best upside gains. Another point is that by the time sufficient investors become involved to cause a stock to rise in price and be recognized, the odds favor some retrenchment as the early buyers begin to sell.

In other words, if you run with the crowd – and the temptation is great – the odds will be against you on a year-to-year basis, unless you are devoting most of your time closely following the activity of the stock market.

CHAPTER 3: FACTORS AFFECTING THE STOCK MARKET

You may wonder why this chapter, as well as the next, should be read before Chapter 5. After all, I did promise you an investment recipe, and that is the reason for writing this book in the first place. However, I believe you will never accept the concepts for the trading of stocks without a basic knowledge of factors that influence the prices of those stocks to go up and down.

I would also like you to be aware that the stock market is a meeting place where financial groups, business activity, and other events combine into a mishmash of conflicting factors. You should recognize that periods of confusion and uncertainty are often your allies, because it will be the pushes and pulls from these many sources that move the prices of stocks. Out of this situation, one thing does become clear – don't join this state of confusion. Just accept that all these factors, and others that you will no doubt observe on your own, will be a way for you to persevere and win in the market.

One thing I have learned in a lifetime of work is not to try to give scientific credibility to any area that defies logic. You have probably already observed that the variations of stock prices are affected by economic cycles, world events, and monetary factors. Then there are some inherent factors in the market itself that make it even more fascinating.

It is nearly impossible for the large number of investors to use all these inputs of information effectively in the market. Most of the time, you will only see the result of some factor on the price of a stock after it occurs. On occasion, you might try to anticipate with an educated guess, that something will happen in the market, but you are still basically guessing. And guessing is not a valid investment tool.

At this stage of my investing life, I have given up trying to make predictions in the stock market. I believe it was J.P. Morgan, who in answer to a query about which direction the market was going to take, replied, "all I know is that it goes up and down." It was always difficult, but during recent years it has become even more difficult for anyone on a continuous basis to weigh all the factors in order to make correct investment decisions.

What this means is that you should be aware that it may take only one of many factors to affect a stock price. It might be the death of the Chief Executive Officer of a company, an announcement of reduced earnings for the last quarter, or any number of news items that can occur. Is the new stock price reasonable? Usually not – the price change has reacted to a perceived change in the fortunes of a company when it actually only signified an emotional response to one factor.

For that reason, I suggest that you stay alert to the many times in the stock market when the stock price is out of kilter with what is reasonable. Those times present both buying and selling opportunities on the change in the stock price alone and not whether you know a whole spectrum of complex factors.

The technique of investing that I suggest for pension plans derives its main benefits by looking ahead and anticipating that some news is bound to come along to affect the stock price. The technique anticipates that some good news will trigger a rise in the price of the stock after you have made the purchase. It also anticipates that once the rise in the price has occurred, some bad news is sure to come along eventually to cause stock price to drift back down to former levels. These are two simple factors that I can understand and it makes sense to me. This type of thinking usually places you in and out of a stock earlier than the big bulk of other investors. That is not a bad position to take from the standpoint of a safe investment.

The direction from where the news arrives that might affect the price of your stock is generally never known. But in recent years, a number of factors have become more prominent than others, and the following discussions should be of interest. I will also evaluate each of the factors in terms of how they might aid your decision on whether to buy or sell certain stocks relative to their distinct patterns of prices.

ECONOMIC FACTORS

There are a relatively small number of economic factors I try to keep track of, and they are used primarily to either give me confidence or to let me assume some wariness at some point in time. You, no doubt, have observed some factors of your own. As you read the financial literature, you will see that a large number of economic factors are recorded on weekly and monthly periods. The buying and selling of stocks are sometimes made for factors other than the economic status of the United States, but it sure is nice to see some comfortable signs.

Business Cycle

I believe the business cycle was better defined years ago. Some major business slow-downs lasting up to one and a half years often occurred about every four to six years. The overall stock market trend pretty well followed that pattern.

For a multitude of reasons, I would not count on this type of repetitive pattern now. Certainly, the subtle change toward a service economy has had the effect of stabilizing the business cycles. The computer age has probably helped in keeping track of inventories, and our manufacturing base has contracted somewhat in certain industries, factors which have helped to better match the forces of supply and demand.

In a subtle way, cycles appear to be occurring more in individual groups of stocks than for the broad-based economy. And since you are interested in the ups and downs of individual stocks, getting familiar with what is happening with autos, cement, and paper is sometimes as beneficial as the composite look at the economy.

A perception of good times in the economy usually spells good times for many stocks. In other words, a bull stock market should coincide with a strong economy, while a declining economy should turn stock prices downward. But do not forget – not all the stocks will follow these trends.

The stock market will tend to rise before an economic recovery and will begin to decline before the economy falters. It tends to act as a leading indicator more times than not. This concept should point you toward adding to your stock positions when any recession appears to be at its worse level. You should also begin to sell off more of your portfolio when business appears quite good.

Company Expansion

Companies will tend to expand operations, build more plants, and even purchase other companies when business is good. Any distribution of this news might allow for a beneficial rise in price for its stock. I sometimes look at this news as an area of concern for stock prices rather than undue optimism. If I had already achieved a profit in the stock before the news, I might wait for a further small rise in the price of the stock and then sell.

Especially of concern would be the news of the diversification of a company into areas that are not related to its basic core business. While diversification has some benefits of safety, it often does not add any impetus for a substantial rise in the stock price.

Unemployment Figure

A recent figure that appears to make the stock market react each month is the percentage of unemployment in the country. It now appears that when unemployment goes up, it's good news for stock prices. I would not count on that relationship to hold true over a long time period. The reason it works that way now is apparently tied to whether or not the interest rates will head down if a slow-down in the economy persists.

I do not suggest using this information for buying a new stock, but it may help in deciding whether to lighten up on your portfolio or to hold a stock position for a little more gain. For example, if you held a stock which was interest-sensitive, such as Sears, Roebuck, you might hold off selling and reach for another 5% to 10% gain in net profit if interest rates are declining. The perceived drop in the interest rate appears to carry more weight than either the fact that fewer people are working or that the economy is not robust. But it does make some sense in that investors are now looking ahead and anticipating the benefits of the drop in interest rates on the bond market, as well as to the eventual pick-up of the economy.

Inventory Figures

Any news concerning the build-up of inventory in certain businesses should awaken some caution in your thinking. That specific news may signal an eventual slowing in business activity. For example, if you owned stock in Ford Motor Company and heard there was a 100 day supply of cars available, you might shed some of the stock below the price you were hoping to achieve.

Competition

An industrial group that has significant business competition must be watched a little more carefully. Automobiles and computers for example, can show rapid price changes in their stocks. You should be careful to buy these highly competitive stocks near their low points of share prices, during any part of their business cycle.

It is sometimes advantageous to be alert to competition worldwide as well as domestic. Try to think about the long-term implications of certain businesses. For instance, the domestic cement industry has been undercut by foreign competition while the economies of these other countries were depressed. When the economies of the other producing countries begin to grow, the domestic cement companies will probably improve their profit picture. The same conditions hold true for the steel industry.

Build-up Demand for Product

You can usually begin to get interested in the auto stocks after you hear about a couple years of low sales for automobiles. This thinking also holds true for the cement and construction industries as well as others. In other words, the longer period of time that road and bridge building is delayed, the better the recovery should be for these industries. Just think of the new airports and new power plants that should be built in this country within the next ten years.

It is difficult to forecast what might happen, and do not get too cocky, but there is nothing wrong in leaning toward certain groups of stocks because of a perceived timing. The old phrase, "every dog has his day," has a little common sense going for it.

Deficits

I cannot even fathom a guess as to how the federal deficit will play out in the next ten years. Until some resolution is seen rather clearly, I suggest keeping a sizable cash position in your portfolio during most of this period of time. This would be prudent, but do not think the stock market will not be a good place to invest in during this chaotic time. In fact, the variations of stock prices that may occur during periods of financial uncertainty can be especially advantageous for trading in a tax-deferred portfolio.

Inflation

Stocks will normally benefit from a low level of inflation. But levels appreciably over 5%, could take a toll on prices for most of the stock groups. With inflation hovering at the 5% level, I suggest always holding a significant amount of cash in reserve, along with a well-diversified stock portfolio.

Consensus thinking for years was that you should not retain much cash during an inflationary period of time. In practice, that thinking does not always work out. Economic conditions can change rapidly in either direction. If inflation worsens, then stock purchases can usually be made at even lower prices. The paradox is that a number of stock prices could decline in either the inflation or deflationary situations, or some stock prices could rise in either of the two economic periods. I never told you it was easy.

The interplay between the inflation rate and economic factors is often confusing, and just how the stocks are affected by inflation is also confusing. One input to the problem probably occurs when a rapid rise of interest rates causes a drain of money from stocks. Certainly the relatively low yield from stocks is no match at this time against other investments that bear high interest.

From my viewpoint, I still believe that the ownership of companies with a huge asset base are worthwhile, especially when their stocks are purchased at bargain price levels. I also think an inflation environment will tend to keep stock prices seesawing through a pretty good trading range.

WORLD EVENTS

It is hard enough to keep track of the domestic economic events let alone what is occurring elsewhere in the world. But other countries do appear to have a greater input on our economy in recent years than was observed in earlier times. For that reason, keep on top of a few bits of information that arise.

Wars and Terrorist Action

I believe news of military action and terrorist activity has less input on stock prices than some of the other world events. But be more aware of the news out of the Middle East and South Africa because of its effect on oil and precious metal supplies. Usually this type of news will make investors nervous and some sell-offs of stocks may occur. Stocks of some natural resource companies may rise in price during these periods, so if you have any of these stocks in your portfolio, hold on for a little better gain. Foreign wars or upheavals will have a greater effect on some of the multi-national companies, but do not jump too fast.

Interest Rate

One bit of news that affects stock prices, especially out of West Germany and Japan, is whether interest rates rise or fall elsewhere in the world. If foreign rates go up, that tends to put pressure on the domestic financial markets. This situation has been made worse with the high national deficit. The interest rates in the United States will probably have to stay in pace with other countries to help keep money flowing into our country. The question mark will be whether the value of the dollar stays high because of other reasons.

Always remember that the United States has shifted into being a debtor nation instead of a creditor for the rest of the world. Until this changes, the stock market will probably be subject to rapid price movements caused by the sensitivity to the money problems of other countries.

Changes in Europe

The changes in Eastern Europe open up a potential demand that should affect the economies of the well-developed countries. But the changes will probably occur at a slow pace and I cannot see any immediate effect on the broad-based USA stock market. Whatever changes that occur will be positive though, especially if peace exists in that area of the world for the next ten years. Benefits for stocks should be observed more through what may happen with the so-called peace dividend. This might require five to ten years for any real effect to be seen.

MONETARY FACTORS

I do not look for too much information from the monetary indicators because I get confused pretty easily. Since we are in a time period of monetary movements that appear uncertain, do not take the projections and indicators, both optimistic or pessimistic, too seriously. In other words, play it cool with an attitude that believes that just as water seeks its own level, so will the economy.

And can you imagine interest rates not falling as a recession occurs? In those times political, and human pressures will become staggering. As you perceive gloom by others to be at its height, you should begin to get more optimistic about stocks.

I mentioned earlier that money should be considered a commodity. The level of interest rates, as well as its trend up and down, determines the relative cost of borrowing money and has a substantial effect on stock prices. But two bits of information appear to be simple indicators and should help you judge whether it is the right or wrong time to buy stocks.

Cash Holdings

You will hear on occasion that the level of cash reserves has grown in the pension and mutual fund investment firms. Usually this information is not current by a week or two. However it is news-worthy because it should give you greater confidence to hold stocks when the money ratio is considered high, at least above the 10% cash levels. If you note that the money levels being held by professional managers are considered on the low side, you may want to sell a little more of your portfolio.

Interest Rates

It used to be that the weekly reporting of the amount of money held in savings and checking accounts triggered some movement in the stock market. In recent times, any perception of a trend in interest rates will usually cause significant price variations in the market. I do not suggest that you get nervous from all this talk. Just be aware that the recent actions of the Federal Reserve Board have been to fine-tune the economy by using changes of interest rates along with the emphasis on keeping inflation under control. Even a small change in rates can sometimes cause emotional buying and selling in stocks which should allow you a period of good trading activity. The key point is that if the interest rates drift down, then practically all the groups of stocks tend to benefit to various degrees.

MARKET FACTORS

The relationship of economic cycles, world events, and monetary factors tend to intertwine and affect the stock market in a variety of ways. Yet, the stock market also has a life of its own composed of its own factors.

Type of Company Chosen

A good portion of any success that you will achieve in the stock market is based on the specific stock you choose for your investment portfolio. There is no magical way for accumulating the companies that give you enough comfort so that you are willing to place money into their stocks. My definition of a good company for investment is one that you can make money on by trading its stock – stay with these winners over a long time period and try to shed the others as quickly as possible.

Good companies to choose for pension portfolios would have been in business for at least forty years so that they have survived a number of recessions. Companies with a long record of dividends showing a steady increase in the rate of pay-out are good ones to consider. Good name recognition has benefits. Choosing a company with a growing business outlook is recommended.

Look for companies that have large asset holdings. As you survey the tabulations that rate the financial statistics of companies with others in the same industry group, look for companies situated no less than half-way down in the tabulation. Most of the companies I recommend for a tax-deferred portfolio would probably be listed on the NYSE – but that does not exclude quality stocks on the other exchanges.

You will normally find that the stock of a financially sound company fitting the above description will not have a high degree of price variability.

That feature give you a little peace of mind, but the stock you pick must still have enough of a significant price change for each year to be practical for the purposes of trading. Otherwise, start looking for another company to place into your portfolio.

It has always been amazing to me to observe how many conservative companies will have their stock prices shift from 20% to 50% during a relatively normal 52 week period in the market. An often observed stock swing might be in the range of $17 to $26 or $35 to $50. When a large disturbance occurs in the market during any given year, such as the dip in 1987, the difference between the high and low end of a stock price may reach 100%. Substantial buying opportunities occur with that type of price spread when a cash reserve is available.

The main point is that if you accept the premise that trading stock in mature quality companies has an advantage for the growth of assets in your portfolio, you still have to be able to collect a number of companies whose stock moves up and down with the market. Some of the conservative companies you choose can even show an upward price movement in a down market. So much the better.

A major reason for the choice of large, mature companies in the pension stock portfolio also relates to their dividend yields. The total annual return on your portfolio is made up of the price appreciation of the stocks you hold added to any dividend and interest income that you receive. A goal of an overall 15% return means that you only need a 11% gain on the average prices of your stocks, if the average dividend and interest yield of your portfolio is 4%.

Often your first interest in a company may come from seeing it recommended by advisors or in a financial article. You should then cross check its current stock price against the price range of the last couple years. You should also check its price-earning (PE) ratio for reasonableness when compared to other companies in the same industry group. On balance, the lower the PE ratio becomes in a bear market, the lower the risk becomes from the investment. Historically, a PE ratio range of 8 to 12 is pretty good for the companies you may originally take a position in, especially when the earnings are about twice that of the dividend payment. For example, if a stock price is $30 with a PE of 10, that would indicate earnings of $3 per share. If the dividend payment is 1^1/_2$ per year, then the stock price appears reasonable. Remember that this information, as shown in the daily stock table, refers to past conditions. You must always weigh that fact against some of the other factors that you are observing before a final decision is made for your stock purchase.

I believe you should understand some of the ramifications of the PE numbers as I have perceived them through the years. Normally, a PE range of 8 to 12 usually applies to conservative and mature companies. It is highly conceivable that you will observe PE ratios of 20 to 30 for companies which are expected to grow rapidly. In many cases, these high PE ratios represent the smaller capitalization stocks, but on occasion, will represent a few of the larger concerns. Often the high PE number for the smaller companies will also coincide with little or no dividend payment. In other words, profits are usually returned to the company for potential future growth in its revenues.

Therefore, high PE numbers are often a measure of investor perception that the future bodes well for that company, and that earnings will eventually catch up with the stock price so as to command more reasonable PE values. If you look at the Japanese stock market, perception has almost gone out of sight with PE numbers of 50 to 60 for some of the listed companies. That's a very worrisome condition, and only time will tell what this means. One caution about high PE numbers occurs when the earnings of a large, mature company takes a major decline. This may only be a temporary condition, or it could be an omen of future troubles.

Since much of this book addresses investment in stocks best suited for pension plans, there is a leaning toward established well-matured companies. The reason for this company bias in a trading method is that the revenues of large, mature companies tend to grow at a low rate. This generally means that the yearly variation in the stock price of these companies is affected more by the changes in economic and monetary factors than by earnings – a desirable trait for trading in the same stock year after year. Remember what I deem to be key to the long-term success from trading stocks – specialize in the same stocks over and over again rather than jump from one new stock to another.

An example of a company that fits my profile is Sears, Roebuck – certainly until something happens to drastically change their business situation. Sears – a trading stock? Its last six years would show the following statistics:

Year	PRICE RANGE		PERCENT DIFFERENCE (FROM HIGH)	PE RANGE	
	HIGH	LOW		HIGH	LOW
1989	$48^1/_8$	$36^1/_2$	24%	12	9
1988	46	$32^1/_4$	30	17	12
1987	$59^1/_2$	26	56	14	6
1986	$50^3/_8$	$35^7/_8$	29	14	10
1985	$41^1/_8$	$30^7/_8$	25	12	9
1984	$40^3/_8$	$29^1/_2$	27	10	7

It is always possible that throughout any given year, the Sears stock might go through a couple of smaller cycles of 12% to 18% changes in its price. Even variations of this magnitude present trading opportunities for the tax-deferred portfolio, as long as the buy and sell commission is about 3% of the total cost of the transactions or less than 25% of the gross profit.

I do not mean to imply that the small capitalization stocks (small cap) should be completely avoided. It just means that the large, mature companies better suit the trading method discussed in this book. Small, relatively new companies will generally offer the greatest chance for appreciation as well as for losses, but I do not recommend the purchase of their newly issued stock for the tax-deferred portfolio. You will receive no tax benefits with losses in a tax deferred pension plan.

The smaller company stocks are usually bought for growth in appreciation over a relatively long time period. When you hit one right, the results can be quite rewarding with a geometric growth in the price of the stock. The difficulty of first buying and then deciding when to sell poses a continuous dilemma for the investor. Small cap stocks are usually bought and held until either success or failure occurs with its accompanying periods of either elation or disappointment. Not the type of emotions that I would recommend for the holders of retirement portfolios – especially the emotion that results from a disappointment.

However, I believe that the younger you are, the greater chance you could take with an investment in smaller companies within your retirement funds. But even then for a tax-deferred pension plan where you anticipate trading in stocks, I would keep the portion of small capitalization companies to less than 10% of the stock value of the portfolio. References to a non-pension portfolio of stocks will be discussed in Chapter 7.

Market Cycles

A dictionary definition for cycle that would apply to the stock market would say that it is a period of time in which events tend to repeat. Certainly the table for Sears, Roebuck in the previous section shows a cycle that everyone can understand. The prices of the stock go up and down and form a pattern of familiar numbers. In a practical sense, that type of cycle is one that an investor can employ to good advantage over the years.

There are many different cycles of price variations in the stock market. Some of these cycles may apply to weekly, seasonal, or even multi-year time periods. In some cases, you may hear about patterns of buying and selling of stocks around certain three-day holiday weekends. I do not place any personal emphasis on this type of investing, but many persons evidently do, so you should be aware that it exists. I always work on the theory that if something proves successful, then keep doing it – but my confidence in any cycle other than the one showing the price movements of mature companies has not been too high.

The effect of the business cycle on stock prices is a strong one, but the timing looks like it will be fairly erratic for years to come. Certainly any cycling of interest rates will be seen in the movement of stock prices. Above all, the cycle of a given company's stock price is the one you should be interested in following year after year.

Every stock tends to move within its own cycle based on an inherent supply and demand relationship. For example, stocks are watched by various groups of investors and judgements are then made to buy and sell. But when stocks decline in price, there are simply more sellers than buyers and the decline continues until a balance between these two groups occur. Stock prices then fluctuate around a "support level."

Conversely, if, for whatever reason the price of the stock begins to trend upward, the buyers outnumber the sellers until the number of buyers diminishes and a price level is finally reached that is normally called a "resistance zone." This cycle relationship tends to have a life of its own but is no doubt affected by many of the other factors discussed earlier.

Market Timing

Market timing is a common term that is used in stock market discussions. Everyone would like to know just when to buy or sell stocks based on a prediction of some upward or downward trend of the overall averages. There are a number of diagnostic tools used by a large group of analysts to predict when the right time exists. The stakes are high since about 60% to 90% of all the stocks listed on the market tend to go with the major turn. The task of developing a method to catch these major turns appears to be exceedingly difficult in today's environment. Otherwise, there would not have been so many funds caught at the wrong end of the market in recent years.

In any narrow trading range, probably comprising a 5% to 10% range on the Dow Jones Industrial Average, I believe you will see certain individual stocks or even selective industry groups show much different price variations than others. This trading range of the market has a much greater frequency of occurrence then does a market turn of major proportions. If that holds true, it then appears reasonable to work with an investing technique that utilizes this narrow trading range.

Market Signs

Most persons who get interested in the stock market at some time or other identify some pertinent signs to help in their investment decisions. I tried plotting a few market variables years ago, but found it too difficult to maintain a program long enough to achieve any success. The professional analyst with a full-time emphasis on data compilation should and does search continually for meaningful relationships in the market. However, that does not mean that the success of the professional analyst is a given.

I believe that any investor having some other full-time activity will have some difficulty matching the stock market professional in this complex area of data analysis. If the system you set up is not simple and requires much time, you are sure to give it up somewhere along the line.

Your system should at a minimum allow you to visually pick out the variation of a stock price during a period of several months. If you have more time, you could actually graph the price movement of the stocks over a longer period of time. However, the investing technique that I am recommending is less concerned with a market trend than the ability to pick out where a stock price exists relative to a target buy or sell level.

But as you read the literature and gather in a wide body of stock market knowledge over the years, you will probably find some bits of information that will tend to give you added confidence in your program. I have settled on two sets of market figures, that when combined with some of the earlier factors discussed, add to a small personal assortment of practical investment tools.

Stocks Reaching High and Low Price Levels

One of the key market signs I look for is the ratio of the number of stocks that reach a new high price versus the number of stocks reaching a low point in price for the year on the NYSE. It is a relatively simple way to help you judge whether or not it is a good time to make a transaction in stocks .

For example, a large ratio of highs to lows should make you cautious, while a large number of lows should start to make you think bullish for the purchase of stocks. I believe you can see that the reverse psychology of this ratio helps you stay out of phase with the mainstream of the stock market.

If after one or more days you observe that the stocks reaching new high prices number 200 or more, while the lows number 5 or less, be cautious about purchasisng any additional stocks. These types of ratios would be normally seen in strongly rising markets. This observation is more apt to convince you to sell off some borderline stock at this point in time for a satisfactory gain. The reverse feeling could occur with maybe 200 or more stocks reaching new lows and 5 stocks showing new high prices. This observation, especially if this reverse ratio stays fairly constant over days, should make you become interested in purchasing some stocks if their prices are at bargain levels.

Do not jump on this indicator as a sure-fire sign at first. Learn to glance over these high-low figures at the extreme movements of the stock market and get a feeling for its pattern relative to the stock prices you have in your portfolio. In time, I believe you will use it as I do, as just another confidence factor during emotional times in the stock market. These figures are usually obtained on a daily basis from your local newspaper or television, or can be seen as weekly summaries in other sources.

Volume of Shares Traded

Another market sign that I believe can help guide you in decisions for stock transactions is the amount of shares traded on the NYSE. The number of shares, easily obtained by radio, TV, or newspaper, has grown through the years as the market has grown. But the number of total shares traded should stay within a reasonably stable range that may last for at least several years in duration.

For example, during the 1989 - 1990 period, a range of 120 to 200 million shares traded per day usually coincided with reasonable price movements in the market. The Dow Jones Industrial Average (DJIA) might shift from 2 to 30 points easily in either direction during each day without exceeding 200 million shares. These figures are not considered out of line and should not present any concern to the investor.

However, a major drop in the DJIA of over 50 points during any one day with a volume of trading over 200 million shares should trigger a little interest. If this pattern continues and volumes increase well over 200 million shares, with accompanied larger drops in the Dow Averages, then buying interest is warranted. Single day large drops in the Dow Jones, along with a large number of shares traded, will generally occur when the market has already been ripe for an appreciable downward correction. It is at these times that your cash reserve in your pension portfolio should already be at a fairly high level. As will be noted later in the Recommended Technique, cash levels at 50% of your total portfolio value is a desirable position to have when the stock market has reached high levels. This is especially true after a substantial long-term rise in the averages has already occurred.

If the market averages continue to drop while the number of shares changing hands stays at abnormally high levels, it might still pay to hold off making any sizable stock purchases. Do not act too fast even though stock prices have already reached reasonable buy levels. After all, these times do not occur too often so you want to take advantage of any pendulum effect from panic selling. But as soon as the trading volume of shares return to a range considered normal for that period of time, you should begin purchasing stock to build up that portion of your portfolio.

In other words, you are now using the observation of the reduced volume of shares that are traded as a sign that the selling pressure for stocks has abated. Even though you should be making your transaction decisions primarily based on the prices of the stocks you are following rather than from any other sign, it still is nice to get some confirmation that the time is right to make a transaction.

The reverse action holds true for a rapid rise of the stock market averages when a large volume of shares traded passes the 200 million mark. At times, you might even observe upwards of 300 million or more shares traded. This sort of a buying frenzy should restrain your desire to sell some of your stock positions even though the desired sell prices have been reached. When the daily volume of shares traded returns to a normal range, you should then begin to shed a number of shares that have surpassed your upper sell target for those particular stocks.

In the last analysis, the scenario you undertake at both ends of any extreme move in the market must be one that gives you some comfort. The observation of the level of the trading volume should help in your decisions. And remember not to anticipate that the market will keep going indefinitely in either direction because there is always an inherent drying up of both sellers and buyers at some point in time.

There are also periods of time when light trading volume exists, yet appreciable drops or rises in the Dow Averages still occurs. Do not make hasty decisions during these periods, but rely on your preset targets to help you determine a buy or sell transaction. At these times, be flexible in your judgements concerning stocks, but stay on the conservative side.

When exceedingly large volumes of stock trade downward as occurred on October 19, 1987, it appears reasonable for you to make a fast judgement for the buying of stock. Hopefully your cash position is ample at that time to be able to take advantage of another one of those 600 million share days showing a 500 point drop in the Dow. Why jump in at that point? Because it's unlikely that more 500 point drop days will occur in a row. Using about half of your cash reserve after a drop of this proportion is not a bad strategy.

While I suggest that the figure for the total volume of shares traded on the NYSE can be used as a simple indicator, it is also possible to keep track of the number of shares that are traded for each stock you are following. In an effort to simplify the investment technique and keep the time spent per week to a minimum, I did not pursue this type of record keeping. Many times too many figures can confuse instead of enlighten. I could not conclude too much years ago when I plotted share volume versus the changes in stock price. But that does not mean that this approach, as well as other techniques that employ volume statistics, will not provide a relationship that may make some sense for you to explain the movements of stock prices. Whatever you ever do, keep it simple so that you have the incentive to stay with a tracking system for a very long period of time.

Market Averages

There are a number of daily figures that refer to the level of prices of shares that are traded on the three exchanges. The DJIA serves as a highly visible barometer for all the market trends, even though it only represents how thirty large company stocks are reacting in the NYSE market. The DJIA is probably the oldest of the averages, and is still an effective indicator because of its wide use in the various information media.

I believe you could buy and sell individual stocks on a daily basis without knowing anything about the averages of the overall market. But from a practical basis, you would lose a sense of the sentiment of that wide body of other investors that helps to shape your decision making in the market. You would also lose that historical pattern of the markets for the good and bad economic times that extends for decades. Picking an average which can represent the type of stocks you are following will give you some background information about how your individual stocks fare against others in the market.

I personally am comfortable with the DJIA, even though it represents only a small number of the companies on the NYSE. These companies represent a sizable bulk of trading each day because of their great number of shares outstanding, and the investor participation in that group. It's prudent to include at least four to five of the DJIA companies into your monitored list of potential stock purchases. Table 3-1 in the Appendix shows the companies that were included in the DJIA as of December 1991 along with the types of values they represent. The Dow Jones Group of averages also includes a transportation and utility grouping and the combination of all three are reported as the Dow Jones 65 Stock Composite.

If that is not enough, you can use the NYSE Index that represents the average of the daily closing prices of all the stocks listed on the NYSE. The Wilshire 5000 is another index which covers the closing prices of 5,000 issues of several exchanges. In addition, there are a number of Standard and Poor (S & P) indices that range from the S & P 500 down to the S & P 100.

Barron's has its own averages and Value Line also has a broad-based index. The Financial News Network, a television financial program, publicizes an index representing a specific group of stocks. And each of the other two exchanges report the daily averages of their stocks in the same way as the NYSE. Usually the DJIA, NASDQ, AMEX, NYSE, and at least the S&P 500 indices are commonly reported each day in newspapers and on the nightly TV wrap-ups of the market. The DJIA is reported frequently throughout the trading day on radio and TV, so it is by far the most visible indicator of the market trend.

You will probably observe that on most major market turns, all the indices are affected somewhat the same way. For example, about the same percentage dip occurred for all the averages on that severe market drop of October 19, 1987. During most of the normal market periods, the trends of all the broad-based averages will generally be similar to the DJIA. But at any period of time, you might see some divergence of the industrial, transportation, and utility averages from each other. At times, the averages for the Over-The-Counter market or the AMEX might even run counter to the NYSE averages.

If you are concerned with making a pension portfolio of stocks grow in value, I do not recommend that you spend too much time worrying about what all the averages mean. I believe you will be well served if you originally concentrate on the DJIA or the S & P 500 as you proceed to gain a feeling for the movements of the market relative to the stocks you are following. The S & P 500 index includes the 30 large capitalization companies of the DJIA as well as 470 other well-established companies. The S & P 500 appears to be a better indicator for the type of stocks you will have because of its large coverage. But as I noted earlier, they will behave with similar patterns during significant stock movements in the market, and those are the times when your investment interest should become more pronounced. For example, compare two periods in the first half of 1990 on the action of these two averages:

	1/19/90	3/16/90	% DIFFERENCE
DJIA	2678	2741	+2.4% rise
S & 500	339	342	+1.0% rise
	4/20/90	6/15/90	% DIFFERENCE
DJIA	2696	2936	+8.9% rise
S & P 500	335	363	+8.4% rise

Note that when the market did not change too much between the January to March period, the difference between the two averages was greater than when compared to the later period of April to June. However, I would not be concerned with some small divergence of numbers like these, especially with a minor change in the market.

If you begin to invest in some of the transportation companies, utilities, banking, or small capitalization companies, then your interest in the other averages would certainly pick up. I generally have stayed away from these groups, but that has been my line of thinking. As you proceed, you could include quality stocks from any group as long as the individual stocks vary significantly in price during each year.

When the DJIA is used as a monitor tool, you will hear comments about a projected percentage drop or rise of the averages during a particular period of time. For example, when a 10% decline happens, and the Dow is at 2900, then you are looking for a drop of 290 points to a new level of 2610. That is considered a satisfactory trading swing for stock transactions. The amount of points dropped or added does not directly represent dollars – even though you may hear it mentioned that way.

Programmed Trading

Recently, a multitude of different ways to invest in the stock market has emerged. I am not sure whether I would call these new techniques unworkable for the average investor, but they sure are confusing to most of us.

From what I gather, there has been a tendency for a number of investors dealing in small amounts of stock per trade to desert the market. I do not know what the statistics are, but enough qualified people have said that to make me a believer.

Part of the reason for this desertion of small investors has been laid to the severe volatility of stock prices in the market dating back even before the one day crash on October 19, 1987. But evidently the sharp drop on that day convinced many small investors to throw in the towel for good. Now we hear that the liquidity of the market, fed by the thousands of small traders or investors in past years, is greatly diminished.

While we can agree that some changes have occurred in the stock markets, I cannot agree that the small investor is less able to successfully invest in this new environment of rapid variations of stock prices. The object is to look at what has happened and figure out in a simple manner how you can benefit from the recent gyrations in the market. Look at the glass as being half full instead of half empty.

The major factor for large one day price changes, either upward or downward, is related to an investment technique called Programmed Trading. This method has been made effective by the marriage of the computer to the stock future indexes. The whole process escapes me so I am not even going to attempt to explain what happens during those periods.

I, like you, can only look at the results of 30, 40, or 50 point changes in the DJIA over a period of one hour and marvel at the scene. Even though Dow variations of this magnitude at the present time may only represent a $\frac{1}{2}$ to 1 dollar of actual change in the prices of many of the stocks traded, they still tend to be a significant event. If Programmed Trading was not bad enough, there are an assortment of other investments in the area of Options that add to the volatility of the market. This produces a condition called "Triple Witching," when three index options expire at the same time. It sure is enough to give you a "twitch."

I did not bring you this far into the book so I could throw a curve at you and state that the smaller investors who left the market were probably right in their thinking. On the contrary, I believe the best of times could be ahead for these investors, and I hope this book has a little to do with bringing them back.

I believe that small investors have to align their approach to stock investment along the lines that I am discussing – one that takes advantage of the volatility instead of being frightened by the swings in the market. Too many conservative investors tend to still invest for the long-term gain. This leads them to purchase stocks and watch their portfolio go up and down over time without doing anything about it. Gaining a little confidence, picking up a little discipline, and taking advantage of the volatile price swings are three good ways the small investor can still beat the averages during this era of Programmed Trading. And what better way to trade in a conservative manner than with the pension portfolio where tax consequences do not affect the decision you make on the transaction.

The rapid Programmed Trading induced swings, like the shakes of a minor earthquake, can present a condition for mental stress if you allow it. But similar to what an earthquake produces, the price variations are primarily a corrective action in the market between two sets of values. This action usually occurs during the last hour of a trading day – which can often add to an already falling market or conversely, work to promote an upward trend already in play.

The key point here is not to allow any short-term observation of the market shake your confidence. It sometimes takes years to groove a golf swing, and it often takes time to groove your investing finesse in the stock market. If you happen to be one of the investors who left the market because of Programmed Trading, it is a good bet you were not too happy with the results of your previous investments. I hope this book will guide you into some new ideas that you can use successfully. If you are considering the use of stock investment for the first time, keep the above thoughts in mind about not losing your confidence prematurely.

Programmed Trading, or any other technique that surfaces over the years, cannot destroy the fundamental premise that stock prices always go up and down in some fashion, even as an underlying market trend takes place. Whether it was in the year 1890 or being projected to the year 2050, the stock market, if it is to exist, must translate its success to the fact that an assortment of buyers and sellers will judge the value of a stock differently. That is really all Programmed Trading is, only it is done with leverage, and the small investor should ride along with these movements and enjoy the scene.

To take advantage of Programmed Trading, you must have an idea of what type of stocks are most involved. The stocks listed in the larger company indices like the DJIA, S & P 500, and S & P 100 tend to contain the stocks of most of the mature concerns. When you develop your investment portfolio of stocks, you will probably find that some company stocks will gyrate more with Programmed Trading activity than others. That is not a bad grouping of stocks to collect.

The object is to stay with a disciplined investment philosophy, with or without Programmed Trading, and still let your buy and sell strategy be based on the reasonable transaction levels you have targeted. Programmed Trading itself should actually speed up the frequency of some of your trades – and there is nothing wrong with that situation. In other words, if your trade is consummated, you are doing so for a reason that you have prejudged rather than allowing your emotions to dictate the action.

Institutional Stock Holdings

Many years ago, I heard that any stock with high institutional participation should be avoided. I believe that type of thinking was geared mostly to the small investor. In today's environment, I actually look for stocks with high institutional positions as being the best type to own in a small pension plan. This group of stocks offers the best opportunity to trade for reasonable profits over the course of a year.

Investment companies, banks, college endowments, and other financial institutions that comprise the large groups that are tracked by Standard & Poor and others, deal with about the same types of stocks that you should be interested in owning. Stocks with high institutional ownership tend to be more financially sound than others and certainly have more outstanding common shares for liquidity in the market.

So an institutional ownership of 50% to 60% of a common stock makes me feel better than if only 20% of the stock is accounted for by that group. One reason for this confidence is that the institutional fund managers and advisors tend to see the same analyst reports about the same point in time. If many of these institutions either buy or sell an ample amount of a specific stock based on these recommendations, then an effect on its price is likely to occur. You will be more likely to be successful if your trading habits are the opposite of those of the institutions.In recent times, institutions appear to be trading more frequently so this turnover action also tends to shift the direction of stock prices.

Some of that up and down pressure on large capitalization stocks must be affected by the on-going battle to pick the right portfolio by the group of managers paid to perform. You should be able to benefit from this activity as long as you are dealing in the same stock grouping as the institutions. A lot of the stock transactions in institutional portfolios tend to occur more often at the end of each reporting quarter, so be especially alert to the price changes at the end of March, June, September, and December.

Superimposed on the institutional and pension plan activity is the large Mutual Fund Industry. The monies being poured into these funds should continue to produce a substantial interest for the high liquidity stocks of the large capitalization companies. As a small mutual funds grows, it must buy larger blocks of shares which direct it to the liquid stocks of the larger companies. So like it or not, your investment in the larger companies, along with the institutions, appears to be prudent for the conservative investor of retirement funds.

For example, the institutional stock holding of a sampling of companies is shown in the following table. This information was obtained from the 1989 year-end stock guide of Standard & Poor. Other publications also contain this type of data for use in your decisions.

INSTITUTIONAL STOCK HOLDINGS

COMPANY	Number of Institutions Involved	Number of Shares Held by Institutions X 1000	Number of Total Shares Outstanding X 1000	% of Total Shares Held By Institutions
Apple	522	86,502	125,681	69
Baxter, Intl.	590	144,037	248,620	58
Ford	864	255,855	473,900	54
Gen. Cinema	228	29,139	68,626	42
Sears	745	177,611	342,402	52
Witco	124	13,703	22,527	61

SYNOPSIS

Divergent factors and multiple market signs generally cause more bewilderment than enlightenment unless you are willing to devote full-time to the investment of stocks. If you are like me, you do not want to work forty years to then saddle yourself to another full-time job so that you can protect your retirement funds. Of course, you can always allow others to direct your investment goals, and this is being done for persons without confidence in the world of stocks. Mutual Funds and Financial Advisory Services provide one way to go, and some element of success has been achieved with this approach. But the self-directed pension plans, including the IRA accounts, are easily set-up to allow the individual investor full control over directing its assets for growth.

For you to be successful in the investment of stocks for your retirement fund, you have to keep uppermost in your mind the key concepts discussed so far in this book. Briefly:

- Develop the confidence that no one has a sure-fire handle on the stock market and that you have as good a chance as anyone to be successful.

- Keep your investment goals reasonable, and don't become greedy in your approach to the stock market.

- Develop a conservative, simple method of stock investing that can last for years, and be built upon. This approach has a much greater chance for long-term success than jumping from one investment technique to another.

- Be comfortable with the stocks you acquire in your portfolio. Know ahead of time when these stocks should be bought and sold.

- Be aware of some of the factors that affect stock prices but do not become enamored with their ability to predict the direction of stock prices. Use these factors as confidence tools when you decide to buy and sell your stocks.

- Keep sight of the primary concept of stock movements - that the prices always tend to go up and down over any given period of time.

- Use market cycles to your advantage. Raise cash at market highs by selling stocks and buy stocks at market lows. But always remember it is the stock you are primarily following and not the market itself.

- Invest the opposite of emotions in the stock market. Know that rash judgements will often be counter-productive for investment success.

- Enjoy the process of directing your own portfolio. Just making money is not enough of an incentive, I say with tongue-in-cheek.

The next chapter will go over some of the methods of investing that should add to your further understanding of the market.

CHAPTER 4: METHODS USED FOR STOCK INVESTING

If you have had some exposure to the stock market and are confused by the variety of recommendations – join the crowd. That is what makes the market so fascinating. At the same time, fascinating activities get old fast when you are losing money. The object of this chapter is to make you aware of the basic methods and philosophies used by a countless number of practitioners of the stock market.

RANDOM WALK

There is a whole group of investors who believe that the price movements of the stock market fluctuate without any set pattern. B.G. Malkiel in his book, "A Random Walk Down Wall Street," basically promoted that position and stated that a Buy and Hold strategy in the stock market should work as well as any other investment technique.

While evidence may confirm that idea at times, you could also present evidence to the contrary. There lies an important concept – that the stock market is a seesaw, complex body of activity, and you should always stay alert to other ways you can invest if advantages are to be gained by this knowledge.

The Efficient Market Theory, in which the prices reflect all the intrinsic value in the stocks, falls in step somewhat with the Random Walk Theory. I have some difficulty with that whole line of reasoning, even though I have no specific data to disprove those theories. It is just hard to imagine that all the investors who buy and sell stock in the market and whose combined action really sets the prices can ever know, as a group, what the real value is of any stock. Even insiders appear to have some difficulty knowing what their own company is actually worth in the marketplace.

In fact, that is why there are buyers and sellers. One group always sees a better value for the stock than what its price indicates, while the other group of investors believe the price is too high. Moreover, the prime way to earn profits on stock transactions is by picking the stock at the right time counter to the action of other investors.

A belief in the Efficient Market Theory would tend to work against you psychologically and keep you from buying a stock when its price is low. That theory basically says that the inherent value of the company at that time is low – and so why buy? Even worse, if you believed the theory to be true and that the high stock price you are observing meant a truly high value of the company really did exist – why not buy? In practice, I believe you are treading on thin ice if you do not buy at the lower end of stock prices and tend to sell when these stocks reach their higher price levels.

Probably a better belief for most investors might be called the "Inefficient Market Theory." This type of thinking says that the price of the stock is mostly out of kilter with the true value of the company.

However, if you really begin to believe that there are random movements in the prices of stocks, then the element of luck could become important. The late Malcom Forbes, of *Forbes Magazine*, years ago recorded the success of a Dart Throwing Investment Technique in which ten stocks were picked by darts landing randomly on a newspaper sheet of stock listings. These ten stocks out-performed the investment results of many other groups during a fixed period of time. Of course, Mr. Forbes coyly stated that the Dart Throwing Technique may not repeat the success of past performances.

I would like to believe that you make your own luck in the stock market. Where so many factors contribute to the end result, I would subscribe to the theory that a little unpredictable luck does not hurt. However, let's look at some of the methods that attempt to minimize the impact of luck.

FUNDAMENTAL ANALYSIS

The use of fundamental analysis for choosing which stocks to buy and sell means that you basically look at all the pertinent financial knowledge of the company. It makes a lot of sense to know the financial health of a company and its business outlook before you invest money into its stock. After all, you would not do otherwise if you considered buying the company outright, and buying its common shares is doing just that on a partial basis.

Just what constitutes fundamental analysis is based on both the fixed factors and the factors that are also subject to your own perception. Some of the fixed factors to consider for companies would include its growth of revenues, earnings growth, debt, assets, dividend record, return on equity, number of shares owned by institutions, price-earnings ratio, and the record of the high and low stock prices reached for the most recent year, as well as for previous years. You could also consider how the specific company you are interested in compares with the other companies in the same line of business.

Out of that whole group of factors to consider about the company, knowledge of the range of its stock price is the most important. The yearly price range is the easiest information to attain and understand. It is not that you do not want to understand all the financial details of a company, but as a practical matter, it is often difficult for most investors to do so.

Some of the subjective things I would look for – and I still call this a part of fundamental analysis – is the visibility and reputation of the company. For example, if two companies had similar financial records, I would generally lean toward the one that is most referred to in magazines and newspapers. If you purchase any products of the company, what is your perception of its quality? In the case of a retail merchandise company, what is their customer service regarding complaints or guarantees? If you feel comfortable with their advertising or public sponsorships, you may have company with other investors.

The key to fundamental analysis, or any other investment analysis for that matter, is to monitor on an on-going basis the changes in the financial health or business outlook of the company. That is easier said than done. It is easy to read from the past records of a company how business has been. But it is often difficult to foresee the surprises that could crop up in what often is an exceedingly short period of time.

One of the reasons I recommend following the same companies for many years is to minimize surprises – but even that is no guarantee of immunity from the unknown. A safe approach might be to mentally anticipate an adverse surprise that could occur in the future of that company after you have purchased its stock. This mode of anticipation should help you get out of the stock after you have achieved a reasonable profit.

Any surprise for a company after its stock has appreciated to a high point will tend to cause the greatest fall of price in a very short time period. Taking profits early is a good technique if you want to play it safe. On the other hand, purchasing stock near its historic low is also a good move because the low support price probably indicates that some depressing surprise had already occurred. In fact, the revolving surprises that usually occur even for well-financed, mature companies is the stuff that dreams can be built upon – because the seesaw affect on prices is tailor-made for profiting from trading activity.

TECHNICAL ANALYSIS

I am not too familiar with the art of pure technical analysis, which appears to take no cognizance of fundamental factors and may not even be concerned with the business of the company. Usually the patterns of stock prices are plotted on charts that are used to forecast the possible next trend in the price of the stock.

Although there appears to be a common language for some of the patterns that show up, technical analysts who use a chart technique fine-tune their own method to help predict the optimum buy or sell level of a stock.

The chart patterns do have some rationale if you consider that the zig-zag price movements tend to represent the accumulation and then distribution of the stock during cycles of activity. The ability to detect the support and resistance levels of a particular stock can help identify possible buy and sell levels. In fact, there are books that outline the concepts of this charting technique as well as companies who distribute charts on a subscription basis.

There appears to be a lot of doubt that this method of charting alone has worked consistently enough to make it the sought after answer for investment success. Everyone would have gone to it by now, if this type of analysis were very successful.

Another chart pattern that is technical in nature shows how a moving average of a stock price compares over an extended time period to the pattern of its daily or weekly stock prices. While this can be done in tabular form, the line chart is most commonly used. The most commonly used time frames appear to be either for periods of 200 days or 13 weeks.

Along with the use of charts, a number of other indicators are also used in technical analysis. These indicators can take in a wide assortment of statistical stock and monetary figures which are published in reports, newspapers, and magazines. Interested investors and analysts then compare the indicators over a time period until a pattern evolves so as to produce some kind of investment sense. For example, the ratio of stock prices making new highs to new lows may be used as one type of indicator. Another indicator might be the ratio of how many stocks advance relative to declining issues on a daily or weekly basis. That type of indicator is often seen in graph form as an Advance/Decline Curve.

Other indicators might follow the trend of specialist short sales and the volume of stock shares being traded. These are but a few of possibly scores of indicators that can make up a program of technical analysis. How much weight to place on each indicator as to its worth in picking stocks or a market trend makes for a difficult decision.

Probably every large investment group will be following a great number of different monetary, economic, and stock market indicator values to help determine market turns on a week-to-week-basis. Advisory letter writers especially develop an assortment of in-house indicators that serve as the cornerstone of their specific service. The difficulty is analyzing what the great number of indicators are trying to tell you. It is not easy, but the quest goes on to pin down either the direction of the market or that of a particular stock.

COMBINATION ANALYSIS

I believe that most stock market analysts use some combination of fundamental and technical indicators. You already know that the stock market can fool anyone. That is why most professionals will use every indicator they can to track trends to cut through this confusion of the market. After all, it is their livelihood, and the stakes are high.

For that reason, utilizing some aspects of both the fundamental and technical analyses makes sense to me. Some of the factors discussed in Chapter 3 showed a sprinkling of both methods of analysis in a very simple presentation. As you read the literature, you may want to add a few more indicators in time. But I really recommend the minimum infusion of data as you start out with an initial portfolio of stocks.

Stick with a successful approach by all means, but do not hesitate to acquire some knowledge about the various analysis techniques as your portfolio grows in size. Just proceed slowly with the accumulation of ideas, theories, and indicators, always being careful to build upon any success you have achieved. Never forget that trading in stocks is not much different than the development of finesse in any other endeavor. It is a time-oriented program, where the fundamentals of what you are trying to do is first simply understood, and then success comes from the doing.

MUTUAL FUNDS

The growth of the mutual fund industry in the last twenty years has been phenomenal. There is no doubt in my mind that mutual funds have weaned a large percentage of the small investors from dealing directly with individual stocks. The concept is valid; co-mingle the money received from many investors into one large fund that is professionally managed. This large pool of money can be distributed among a wide assortment of stocks from different industries to produce the type of diversification that the individual investor would find hard to match.

An assortment of stock funds are available that invest all the way from large capitalized companies to newly-formed, small capitalized companies. There are funds that specialize in select industry groups, utilities, bonds, as well as money market funds. Practically all of the large mutual concerns will allow you to transfer assets between the various funds that they direct.

Mutual funds can be purchased by working directly with the fund company itself or through a broker. There are two basic types known as the no-load or load funds. The no-load funds do not take a commission but usually charge an annual percentage of about 1% of your assets as its management fee. The load funds, usually the type obtained through brokerage houses, can either take an up-front commission or redemption fee as well as receive an annual management fee. You should be careful to check the fees and other expenses of each fund, remembering that it is the investment success of the fund that is most important.

I suggest that if you start to invest in mutual funds that you use the philosophy contained in this book. This will allow you to invest your retirement funds in a methodical manner in the fund and hedge that investment against a cash position. Remember that the mutual funds that invest in stocks are not immune to the ups and downs of the market, so the technique of Chapter 5 can apply as well to mutual funds. See Chapter 7 for some additional thoughts about investing in mutual funds.

Some may need that initial experience with mutual funds so that they can later move into their own stock portfolio with much greater confidence. Other persons might just be comfortable enough with the investment techniques outlined in the next chapter so that they will move directly into the trading of individual stocks.

I tried the mutual fund route for a couple years and personally found it a little more inhibiting and less fun than handling a portfolio of individual stocks. Some mutual funds produce a great record, so if you pick the right ones, there is no doubt that you could do as well financially as you can with your own portfolio. I have become more comfortable working with the same mature companies, year after year, and found that the trading of their stocks have produced a safe and satisfactory return on my retirement assets.

Mutual funds annually distribute their income and net capital gains from the transactions in their portfolio. This distribution can be taken in cash or reinvested into the shares of the fund. It is highly recommended that the distribution always be reinvested so that any growth can be compounded in your retirement portfolio.

The only caution I will leave you with concerning mutual funds is that most funds often keep little money in reserve. During market declines, the subsequent losses in the fund you hold might be greater then you expect. If you always keep a portion of your own investment program in cash at the market tops, you should have little need to worry about that situation.

STOCK ADVISORY SERVICES

Anyone who offers comments on the pros and cons of individual stocks, or the market as a whole, can be considered an advisor of sorts. Professional advisors are available who provide this service for varying fees. I do not envy their profession since predictions must be made continually in a field that is known for its uncertainty.

Yet, because of this well-established uncertainty, the advisors do not appear to lose their credibility when they are wrong in their predictions. If you heard it was going to be sunny from your favorite weather forecaster and your picnic was rained out, chances are that you would still return for the next forecast. You also have to give the predictors of the stock market a break along the way. The only public advisor who may lose some credibility at times is usually associated with an "All or Nothing" approach in their predictions. Being right in this case makes you a hero, and being wrong produces a lot of disappointed investors.

The advisor can offer public advice through an established investment firm, or work as a freelancer through periodic financial newsletters. Most of the established advisors are registered with the Securities Exchange Commission, and they conform to certain ethical standards set by the commission. There are over fifty advisory services that have a wide distribution of publications and have developed a reputation among themselves as well within a sizable group of investors.

The profession of financial planners has become quite visible in the media in recent years. This group of advisors are not being discussed as part of this section since they normally supply a broad - based investment service to individuals or groups on a one-to-one basis. I believe these advisors can perform a useful service to help identify valid ways to allocate money for persons in need of this direction. This type of help is especially suited for the use of personal funds where tax consequences have to be weighed.

The stock market letter writers perform a useful service to the many stock investors who need guidance and confidence in the marketplace. Some of these advisory services refer to economic factors, but most will include their own group of charts, tabulations, and language to help predict the turns or direction of the stock market. Most services will include specific stock recommendations and provide some follow-up for these stocks. Some of the newsletters also monitor the thinking of other advisory letters, and this information provides enlightened comments on the underlying currents in the market.

Even knowing how bearish or bullish the bulk of advisors are at any given point in time appears to be a reasonable investment tool. For example, if a high percentage of the advisors are bearish, that is, they have recommended to their clients to sell stocks, then this fact is determined to be bullish for the market. At first glance, the concept looks screwy. But the reason it may hold water is that if advisors do have some influence in the stock market, then their sell advice has already helped to drive prices down and has therefore placed cash into the hands of active investors.

I do not know if I buy that particular theory, but I do remember when advisors with strong reputations have caused stock markets to rise or fall somewhat by a public pronouncement. So advisors are listened to because they spend their time trying to read the market signs and some of their letters are closely followed by brokers and influential investors.

Is it worth for you to spend $150 to $300 per year on a newsletter to sample the opinion of usually one person? For a number of years I thought so because I found the letters informative and a good way to get a feel for the market. Some of my investment confidence had to come from reading a countless number of letters. These writers develop views and presentations not usually seen in other financial publications.

The following example of the type of advisory opinion that occurs was taken out of the June 25, 1990 issue of *Barron's*. The quotation found on the "Market Watch" page is a small excerpt from the June 15, 1990 issue of the *Professional Tape Reader*, written by Stan Weinstein.

"It's great that the Dow hit another new high this week but what isn't making headlines is the dramatic shrinkage that is taking place in the number of stocks that are hitting new yearly highs. All the way back on May 22, there were 117 new yearly highs registered on the New York Exchange while the Dow was about 100 points lower than the high it reached this week. And since then, fewer and fewer stocks on the New York Exchange have been making the new high list even though the DJIA has punched much higher. That tells us two things. First, that near term market is slowing upside momentum and is likely to soon correct; and second, that this is still a very split tape with both pockets of strength and weakness coexisting side by side."

Now you may not agree with what Mr. Weinstein or any other letter writer might say, but you will not be disappointed over a long period with some of the market insights you will gather from their remarks. Some of the other advisor names you might have seen in print over the years would certainly have included Ned Davis, Norman Fosback, Al Frank, Joe Granville, Bob Gross, Yale Hirsch, Stephen Leeb, Robert Precher, Richard Russell, and Martin Zweig. If you get involved in subscribing to investment newsletters, you will find yourself becoming familiar with many of the well-quoted advisors in this area of financial activity.

Most of the advisory letters will attempt to read the trend of the market, but you still have to own some stocks before you worry too much about the direction of the market. A number of the letters will recommend stock picks either on a letter-to-letter basis or as an on-going portfolio. This source of stock picks might be of interest to you, but I would still recommend some caution for the tax-deferred portfolio.

There is a tendency for most of these advisory letters to stress the smaller capitalization companies rather than the large, mature companies. While the small cap stocks have the greatest chance for large appreciation gains, they also can produce a bumpy price ride. However, some of the letters will also include a number of well-known companies and you might be comfortable with those selections. These advisors will generally provide a buy, hold, or sell recommendation on the stocks in their portfolio for each issue of their letter.

So this is another way you can get started in the stock market. Instead of making the transaction decisions yourself, the letter writer will make it for you. If you choose to look at this approach as a method of investing, I offer two suggestions:

1.   Spend about a year subscribing to a couple of newsletters and follow their philosophy and stock picks during this period without committing any money to their recommendations. Let your money grow safely in a money market fund during this evaluation period.

2.   Pick one of the services you are comfortable with and begin to use their recommendations on a conservative basis. That is, if the recommendation is for a 100% invested position, I would stay with about a 50% cash position depending on the caliber of the stocks. If the recommendation is to sell all the stock, I would probably sell no more than half of the portfolio. In other words, you are betting with the advisors – but not completely. If they are right, you will make a lower return on your investment. If they are wrong, you have still turned out pretty well. That is the way I would play it, depending on the confidence you have in the advisor.

While I can recommend the use of an advisory letter, I must caution you from becoming a "financial newsletter addict." There are individuals who subscribe to numerous letters at the same period of time and then become torn between all the various choices that surface. I call that "the Big Menu Syndrome." But if you enjoy reading the divergent opinions – go for it. Most of the newsletter services provide free issue trials upon request.

Identifying a trend in the stock market is no easy task. For example, the TV show, "Wall Street Week with Louis Rukeyser," presents a sampling of opinions for a market trend six months out from ten well known advisors. The July 6, 1990 show produced the results of 2 Bullish, 6 Neutral, and 2 Bearish. Now that is the kind of stuff that makes decision-making in the stock market so fascinating.

There is even an advisory service that evaluates the recommendations of other letter writers. This evaluation can be obtained from the *Hulbert Financial Digest*, and it's editor, Mark Hulbert, has been one of the regular columnists in *Forbes Magazine*. His comments might provide some knowledge about the advisors with the best track records.

DOLLAR COST AVERAGING

For many years a well-touted method for investing in stocks has been called Dollar Cost Averaging. The theory is simple, and the arithmetic somewhat works in favor of the investor over a long period of time. Therefore, you should understand its benefits as well as its drawbacks.

The use of Dollar Cost Averaging means simply that you invest a fixed amount of dollars at a repetitive time period into the same group of stocks or mutual funds. If you invest $2,000 each May 1st into the same equity investment, the number of shares that are purchased is fixed by the price of those shares at that point in time. In other words, you would buy more shares for your money when the price per share is low, and conversely, receive fewer shares when the price per share is high.

The overall trend of the stock market has been upward even though price set-backs tend to occur along the way. The rationale of the dollar cost method is that at some future time when you want to cash in, the share price of your portfolio holdings should be higher than the average cost of the shares that were purchased during the years of investment.

The advantage of Dollar Cost Averaging was deemed to be its use of a mechanical mode of investing which forced you to buy regardless of market conditions. In theory that was nice, except the investor still had to overcome some emotional resistance to buy when gloom in the market was rampant. My belief is that if the investor has sufficient discipline to invest at a fixed point in time each year (or any other set period of time), that same investor should have enough discipline to do even better in the stock market.

THE BROKERAGE HOUSE

The stock market and the brokerage house becomes an inseparable pair for most investors who buy and sell stocks. The brokerage house can mean many things to different persons, but it primarily acts as an agent for the investor in all sorts of investment activity. I will stick to the activity of stocks.

The large firms are well-known by their advertising messages on television as well as in print. These large brokerage firms are generally part of even larger financial institutions where stock brokerage is just one phase of their business. When the term "Large" is applied to brokerage firms, it usually means scores of retail offices spread out across the nation. It is these retail offices which are usually familiar to the individual investor.

Large brokerage firms have been headquartered in New York City in past years. The accounting statements for their regional offices are usually done at the central site. In addition to these large, well-publicized firms are a number of secondary brokerage companies that have numerous offices about the country. Then there are the smaller regional firms that may limit themselves to six to twelve offices in a specific geographical area. Most of these smaller firms are considered to be full-service brokerage houses.

In recent years, the so-called discount brokerage companies have become quite prominent for the stock investor. These concerns charge a reduced commission on a stock transaction because their overhead is generally lower than the full-service companies. The offered services of these discount concerns will vary greatly from company to company so that you can pick from a wide choice.

Whether you require a full-service or discount brokerage firm really depends on your investment philosophy. The full-service operation will usually supply you with more investment alternatives and advice than the average discount house. Part of the overhead costs of the full-service group involves the analysts and research personnel used to track the market and individual stocks. This information is channelled to you by way of periodic letters and reports. In general, the discount house will not have this type of in-house expertise, but they can, of course, provide a certain amount of guidance from other sources.

The big difference between the two brokerage house types is the commission charge per stock transaction. There is a wide range of fees depending on the number of shares traded and their cost per share. On average, you could probably expect to see the full-service house fees about twice that of the discount firms.

During the 1989–1990 period, a full-service firm might charge you 3% to 4% commission for a single transaction of 100 shares with a per share price of about $20. The moderate discount house charges would generally be found in the $1^1/_2$% to 3% range for this type of trade. As the dollar amount of the transaction goes up, the commission rates will generally trend downward.

A reasonable round trip commission would be a range from 3% to 4% for stock transactions in a pension plan where no tax liability is incurred on the profit of the trade. This range of commissions might steer you toward the discounted firm. However, the full-service firm might also give you a discounted commission if you are considered an active investor and make your own decisions. The background of this book will generally place you into that class in time.

Another big difference between the full-service and discount firms might be the caliber of the broker, who acts as the intermediary between you and the stock exchanges. You may or may not be assigned a broker at the discount house but having one can be beneficial if you take an active investing stance in stocks.

One facet of the brokerage house concerns the protection of your securities. There have been improvements since 1970 in how the brokerage accounts are insured against loss, and I will discuss some of the key safeguards of these programs.

There are really two basic ways to process the transaction of the stock. A lot depends on how actively you trade and how confident you become in your program. You can actually receive a paper certificate that shows the number of shares of your purchase, and this certificate arrives by mail after about a 2 to 4 week period of time. This certificate is returned to the brokerage house when the stock is later sold. This procedure has some inherent handling problems that can occur in the process of taking physical possession of the certificate. The other method is to have the certificate held in "Street Name," which means that the stock is assigned to the brokerage house even though you are the owner of record.

I have preferred the use of the "Street Name" method for its simplicity and ease in the trading of stocks. The actual certificates or transfer records are usually held at a security depository company for safekeeping. The information for the transfer of stocks has been done electronically for quite a number of years. Each brokerage house will generally have a computer disk record of your account, and a copy of all the investment activity for the month is sent to each client. This mode of accountability is like that employed by the Mutual Fund Industry.

Any transaction of stock is confirmed by written notice to the client within a couple of days. If the brokerage house maintains a money market fund as part of your portfolio, then cash is automatically withdrawn to pay for a new stock purchase, or proceeds are credited to the fund upon the sale of a stock position. All of this activity information, as well as the receipt of any dividend or interest payments, is recorded on your monthly statement. This whole process works quite well, and it sure beats the concern of sending stock certificates and checks through the mail.

The financial protection of your securities and cash balances are handled in a couple ways by the brokerage firm. An organization called the "Securities Investor Protection Corporation" (SIPC) was founded after 1970. It is a non-profit corporation funded by the member firms. The purpose of SIPC is to protect the clients of any failed firm from losses up to $500,000, which includes $400,000 in securities and $100,000 cash. This protection, while non-governmental, is not unlike the FIDC used for the protection of bank deposits. One question you would then pose is whether the brokerage house you are considering belongs to SIPC.

Another protection for your securities is the amount and type of client insurance that the brokerage company has over and above that of the SIPC. Most larger firms will protect individual accounts for upwards of $2^1/_2$ million dollars. There is nothing wrong about asking for a copy of this insurance coverage for your records.

The Broker

The term broker is still used to denote the person performing stock transactions at the brokerage firm. More often in recent years, the official title of this group of financial agents might be account executive or account representative. Your connecting link to the stock market is through this broker, and this relationship should encourage confidence in all your transactions.

There is no magic formula for matching yourself with a broker to fulfill these requirements. A relative or friend may recommend a name of a broker for you to contact. Another approach is to visit a reputable brokerage firm and discuss briefly your financial position with the manager of the firm. A broker is generally assigned to you based on this initial discussion. The personality and sincerity of your broker must gel properly with your own nature. You may not know this for a fact until after some period of time. You want to have the feeling that the broker has your best interests at heart. It makes good business sense for the broker to promote that situation, but if there is any doubt in your mind, discuss your problems, and if not satisfied, try another broker. Some tips on broker satisfaction would include:

1.   The broker should be readily accessible. If you have difficulty reaching the broker by phone, and return calls take hours, you are in a poor situation.

2.   Any new critical information on the stocks you have taken a position in should be promptly fed back to you.

3.   Any problem with your account that arises should be followed through by the broker promptly.

4.   Any pertinent stock analysis or stock tabulations should be periodically sent to you.

5.   Any telephone transaction orders should be promptly filled without any change in your instructions. For this to occur routinely takes a careful listener on each end of the phone. Get the communication straight between you and your broker before you go too far or costly mistakes could occur.

If you do ask for investment advice from your broker, you must accept any loss as gracefully as you would any gain. The ability of most brokers to be right on their stock picks may have 50-50 odds, and this situation should be recognized early on. However, some brokers will have varying degrees of success and you might achieve overall market gains following their advice.

I prefer a broker relationship where the information of the marketplace is freely discussed, but I develop and make all the stock decisions. This allows me to feel the emotions from the results of the investment, and the broker is protected from any bad feelings. What I am basically saying is that if you have a good broker whom you are comfortable with, don't let the burden of investing affect your relationship.

The broker makes money on the number of transactions per unit time. If you call three times a day and only buy or sell once a year, it would take a big-hearted broker or a close relative to maintain the relationship with you. So the amount of business given to the broker will often determine the extra time devoted to your investment needs. At the same time, I do not believe the broker should continually stress transactlons unless they are compatible with the investment philosophy of the investor. Another problem that some brokers have, and I can feel for them, is their hesitancy to recommend stocks that are currently out-of-favor. You might like the out-of-favor stocks after reading this book, but this is not true for the bulk of investors who are conditioned to expect stocks to move upward in price relatively fast after their purchase.

For example, if a broker recommended a stock in a depressed industry, and the investor sees no movement or, even worse, sees a decline in the price of that stock after a few months, you will probably have one discouraged investor, one discouraged enough to change brokers. So there is a tendency for some broker recommendations to fall within a group of popular stocks that circulate in the investment community during the same period in time. These popular stocks are often given validation by in-house research reports or other analyst sources.

Remember an earlier concept – running with the crowd can be injurious to your investment health. However there are ways to play this game under your own rules that you should find beneficial for the investment of stocks.

CHAPTER 5: THE RECOMMENDED TECHNIQUE

Let's review the underlying concepts that are fundamental to the practical technique for investment in the stock market.

A REASONABLE RETURN

A satisfactory growth on your investments in a pension plan should achieve a net return about three times that of the current inflation rate in the United States. In recent years, that has meant about a 14% to 15% annual return on your investment. This figure will vary over the years, but 15% has been a very desirable goal over a long time period.

DESCRIPTION OF TECHNIQUE

This recommended technique for investing in stocks is fashioned toward a leveraged program of dollar cost averaging that was discussed in Chapter 4. However, the technique of the book suggests that you initially buy stocks only when their prices are near their low levels compared to the previous couple of years. In other words, you are buying stocks in a select manner that is based primarily on price alone and not related to time.

You should be able to take reasonable profits on the sale of your stocks at varying points in time. The cash proceeds from these sales can be used to buy other targeted stocks at their low price levels. Or the cash is held until you can repurchase the shares of the same company appreciably below the share price of the earlier sale. The mature, larger-sized companies that have been around for many years are tailor-made for this type of investment method. You will tend to become a specialist in a small group of companies whose stock prices vary each year within a nearly repetitive range.

SAFETY OF ASSETS

This technique is directed toward the safe build-up of retirement funds within a tax-deferred portfolio of stocks. You should attempt to buy the stocks of conservative companies that have a good financial foundation. Moreover, I suggest that any company that you might include in your portfolio should have many of the qualities discussed later in this chapter.

CONFIDENCE AND DISCIPLINE

You have already read how difficult it is to predict what may happen in the stock market, and it becomes doubly difficult to obtain any confidence by jumping about between different stocks and investment methods. You can gain confidence from a successful investing method that is simple and works well in a repetitive fashion. The recommended technique of this book has those attributes, but it will take discipline on your part to stick with it long enough to gain that success.

I believe you will need at least four to five years to see the full value of this technique. You might be lucky enough to achieve great success during the first year after you start your portfolio, and then find that the second year did not turn out too well because of a collapse of prices in the stock market. Ah, but the following year can bring you right back to your desired average because your portfolio had basically started from a low valuation level. In other words, this technique cannot knock out all the peaks and valleys of investing in stocks, but it is designed to provide you a satisfactory average return over the long term. If you do not become greedy you will find the technique works well because it only relates to the arithmetic movements of stock prices on a year-to-year basis.

TIME REQUIRED FOR TECHNIQUE

You probably will have some difficulty with allotting enough time to all the activities you are interested in during your working years. Yet, it is during these years that a pension fund should grow at a satisfactory rate. For that reason, I have continually shaped a technique for stock investing that requires less time to maintain during those early years.

As your portfolio grows over a multi-year period, and as you reach a more leisure part of your life, you will probably want to spend more time at the task of improving the results of your investments. The technique, therefore, has an accordion aspect that will allow you to adjust the time spent on your portfolio to the time you have available. This increased use of your time and efforts should begin to produce average results near the 20% level, as compared to the 15% annual return that I consider reasonable when you start.

You will need more time in the beginning to develop your initial portfolio. Once the portfolio exists, I do not believe any more than one to two hours per week will be required to monitor the stocks you have chosen and to make investment decisions. You should learn how to use the technique of open orders during the early years when you are busy with your occupation, business, or family growth. The methodology of these open orders will be discussed later.

USE OF PRICE VARIABILITY IN STOCKS

Most mature companies will see their stock prices vary each year from approximately 20% to 50% from their low to high point. Whether this variation in stock price only occurs once per year is based on many factors. Sometimes the whole price cycle may take a full two years.

For example, a stock with a price of $30 in January may drift down to $20 by December of that year. It may require the whole next year for the price of the stock to return near the $30 level. If you utilize the concepts of the recommended method, you would know not to buy at the $30 level, but more near its historic low level of $20. The technique leads you to then sell the stock at some appropriate point as the price rises in the second year.

DO NOT REACH FOR MAXIMUM GAINS

Even though it would be nice to buy a stock at the $20 low and sell at the $30 high of the preceding example, it is extremely difficult to do this on a practical basis. The recommended technique for pension plans actually works quite well on smaller price variations depending on your cash reserves, the size of your portfolio, and the condition of the stock market. By later examples, I will show the rationale of taking reasonable gains in your transactions even though it often involves the frequent trading of certain stocks.

I know I talk about the buying and selling of stocks as though it were an easy task. And it really does become easy, and often too addictive – much like eating from a bowl of peanuts. In fact, one of the psychological pressures you will continually face is the urge to sell a block of shares every time a profit surfaces. You might even begin to parody the humorist Will Rodgers, and think, "I never met a profit I didn't like." But you soon learn to hold back on premature trades until the profit becomes a satisfactory one.

USE OF YOUR CASH RESERVES

The proper use of your cash reserve in the pension plan is the cornerstone of a successful investment program. The normal variation of the stock market takes a trend up or down, or remains stagnant, but unfortunately you will always see that pattern after the fact. A safe approach would indicate that you keep a sizable cash reserve in your pension account. I earlier suggested that a floating cash reserve of between 20% to 50% of your portfolio value would be a good strategy for most stock market conditions. This cash would normally be held in a money market fund as part of your portfolio at the brokerage house.

However, you might stay more around the 50% to 70% cash position as you initially start out with this method of stock investment, certainly until you gain some confidence. The higher cash level is especially prudent when the stock market is considered fairly high as defined by the Dow Jones

Industrial Average. In recent times, that might be any market level over 3000 on the DJIA.

As the stock market drifts down and stock prices become reasonable, you would work your cash reserve down toward the 20% level. You would begin to restore your cash portion back toward the 50% level by selling stocks in a rising stock market. In time, you will develop a better feeling about the sliding use of your cash reserve and how to improve its percentage allocation.

THE CONTRARIAN APPROACH

This technique utilizes a contrarian approach which means that you should be purchasing and selling stocks opposite to the popular positions being taken by most other investors in the market. There are many persons who use this technique of investing, but there appears to be more persons who do not. And that is why the method works.

MONEY INFUSION INTO YOUR PENSION PLAN

The best stock investment ideas will not produce any success without the necessary cash to be able to start a portfolio. While it is possible to begin with a minimum one-time deposit at an early age, and eventually build up a sizable retirement fund, it is not the method of choice. The desirable way to ensure investment success is to continue to make deposits into your portfolio, as often and as much as you can afford, especially during the first ten years of a pension program.

At a minimum, the allowable $2,000 per year should be added to your IRA account, whether or not it is deductible. Just be sure you keep track of its deductible status over the years. You can start an IRA account at a brokerage house as long as you earn some money during the year. You should initiate the IRA even if you have to transfer personal savings to attain the fully allowable deposit into the tax-deferred account.

A wonderful technique for raising tax-deferred money is to start a side business while you are young, regardless of your employment status. This will allow you to set up a Keogh Pension Plan where 20% of your net earnings (as of 1990) can also be sheltered. If you can earn $10,000 extra, that would mean another $2,000 a year could be deposited into a pension plan. Roll the Keogh proceeds into your IRA account when your side business terminates. An important side bonus of these contributions is that they are subtracted from your current taxable income.

If you are employed and are included in a company pension plan, recent pension laws allow you to receive your vested portion if you transfer to another company. This vested money should be rolled right into your IRA account. You can see that most persons can achieve a sizable cash reserve in a self-directed pension portfolio if the goal is properly set.

An incorporation of a business or profession provides even greater options for a self-directed pension plan. These plans especially fit well for persons starting their retirement funds at a later point in life.

The principles of investing outlined in this book apply equally well to the IRA or a company pension plan. The more money you start out with in your IRA or pension fund, the more flexibility and safety you'll have in your investments. An amount of $20,000 would be considered a reasonable base for a stock program in a pension plan. Aside from the sum of money kept for personal emergencies, your first efforts must be to fund your pension portfolio even if you have to place any personal investment portfolio temporarily on hold.

Even though I suggested $20,000 as a starting base, this amount is not etched in stone. It just happens to be a reasonable amount, because a favorable outcome of this technique comes from the balance of a cash reserve against the stock portion of your portfolio. You tend to be slightly limited with too small an asset base.

However, a strategy I suggest if you were starting an IRA account (and contributing annually the full $2,000 allowable), is to utilize the first couple of years for just learning the technique. Explore the ways that I describe in this chapter on how the technique works under the various conditions of the market. This could be done on a paper basis without any actual outlay of cash. You would then be attuned to the characteristics of the companies you have chosen for your paper experimental portfolio, and thus be mentally ready for any actual transaction at a later time. If your confidence becomes high after you have accumulated much less than $20,000, you could initiate a buy program even at the lower cash level.

Let's say you have studied the trends of the stocks you have chosen, and the stock market suddenly collapses to a new low point of the averages observed for the previous couple of years. You might only have $4,000 at this time, but your confidence is high because of the test monitoring you have done. You could go ahead and invest the whole amount of cash into a couple of stock positions which appear to offer the best upward price potential. In other words, you would have taken advantage of the market conditions at the right time with whatever money you had available.

CHOOSING YOUR PORTFOLIO STOCKS

You have just read about ways to use a sufficient asset base so that you can increase your chance for success in a pension plan of individual stocks. Another large part of that potential success is to be able to come up with the right group of companies that should be considered for your portfolio. Do not make this first list of companies a time-consuming ordeal. Just remember that the business and financial aspects of mature companies should fit within some basic guidelines. This means the company has:

1.   Been in business for many economic cycles (over 40 years).

2.   A substantial asset base (over 1 billion dollars).

3.   A long record of dividend payment (over 15 years).

4.   A good current asset to liability ratio (over 1.5).

5.   A low long-term debt to capitalization ratio (less than 50%).

6.   A reasonable price-earnings ratio (less than 15).

7.   A reasonable stock price variation for each year (at least 30%).

8.   Good name recognition.

Some of the companies you chose may only have four to six of the acceptable guidelines and still be considered good candidates for your portfolio. Do not become too immersed in the detailed financial facts of these companies unless your knowledge and confidence is sufficient to be able to handle this type of analysis. The first group of companies that you will pick may not have an air of excitement about them. These relatively large companies may be from the cyclical basic industries, plus some consumer companies that should inject some stability into the portfolio. You also should sprinkle a few lower priced issues in along with the more moderately priced stocks. The stocks that should be considered for a starting portfolio might be best found in the $15 to $50 per share range.

I believe a list of twenty companies makes for a practical number of stocks that you can follow. Table 5-1 in the Appendix shows a list of twenty companies that I felt comfortable with in 1990, and how I tabulated their vital signs. You may be comfortable with twenty completely different companies.

You in effect become a specialist in the group of twenty companies you chose, learning their characteristics and price movements over time. It is not necessary to choose a company for this list just because it happens to be at the low point of its price range. You ideally would like to have a mix of companies where one group of your stocks might be peaking in price when others are in a state of price depression. Table 5-2 shows a comparison of the high and low stock prices for the twenty companies of my list over a four year period.

The companies shown in these tables would not be considered high-growth companies, but that does not mean they could not break out of their historical price range on the high side at any time. One of these companies could be taken over and lose its identity. Or the worse case of all would occur (other than a complete collapse of price caused by bankruptcy) if its stock price would become stagnant for a number of years. In all of the above examples, those companies should be weaned out of your list and replaced with others that fit your plan.

You might own the stocks of three to ten of the companies shown on your list, depending on the size of your portfolio and the conditions of the market. You should still follow the stock prices of each of the twenty companies as though you had purchased all of them. If you cannot cope with the number of twenty then cut it down to a number you can handle with your available time. The more companies you can maintain on your monitor list, the greater number of investing opportunities should show up over time. Feel comfortable in asking your broker for information on an on-going basis for the companies on your list.

DIVERSIFICATION OF THE PENSION PORTFOLIO

The diversification gained by the use of many stocks in a pension plan portfolio is less critical if you make your first purchases in companies that are considered most conservative and somewhat diversified within their own operations. The formation of the initial portfolio should give you a chance to get started slowly without the need to make rapid decisions for transactions.

Internal diversification is often observed with large companies such as Sears, Ford, PPG, Westinghouse, as well as Baxter International from Table 5-1. For example, Sears is involved in retail merchandising, real estate, finance, and insurance. While this diversification provides an air of safety in the investment, it can also dampen the volatility in the stock price of the company. At times, one area of the company's business may be in the doldrums, such as the merchandising segment of Sears, or the nuclear power division of Westinghouse. These segments will often control the level of the stock price of the parent company during any one period of time.

GETTING STARTED

Once you have developed your list of companies, you'll have a base of information to help you make those initial stock purchases. Check how the current price of these stocks relate to the recent historical price records as shown in Table 5-2. Any of these stocks within 10% of their average low price of the last two full years should be considered for purchase first. A work sheet, such as shown in Table 5-3 can be made up to facilitate your efforts.

Choose the companies on your list based on their quality and underlying asset base, not on their timeliness. In other words, you are not prejudging when and how the stock prices will vary for these companies.

This technique eliminates the need to make a buying decision when the market makes a fast recovery. It is easy to procrastinate on stock transactions when the market makes any kind of a turn. That is why it is beneficial to apply some objectives to an investment method.

Those reasonably priced stocks in Table 5-3 that you will consider buying will have to be weighed against the economy, the market level, and how much cash you have on hand. Use some of the earlier discussions for help as you make those first decisions. Certainly it would be nice to wait and buy some of your first stocks at a price 10% below their two-year average low price. But that may not occur because the market could very quickly take an upward turn.

It is therefore prudent, when you are starting out with an investment program, to just go ahead and make a small commitment of cash to one or two stocks that appear reasonable in price at that point in time. Consider that you had developed a list such as seen in Table 5-3, and are ready to start a program on 7/20/90 with $20,000 in your cash reserve. The DJIA was at the 2960 level at this time, which was close to an all-time market high. Talk of recession, inflation, and high and low interest rate changes were rampant in the news media, reflecting a time of nervousness for investors of all kind.

Since you should now be a believer in the craziness of the stock market, you are neither a bull nor a bear. You observe that three companies fall within your buy guidelines – General Cinema, Greyhound (Name changed to Dial Corp. 1991), and Sears. If you proceeded to buy a 100 share block in all three companies, it would consume about $8,400 or 42% of your cash reserve.

You might also reason that since all three of these companies are consumer-oriented, buying the stock of all three at the height of the market would not be prudent. Your decision might be to settle on the two most conservative stocks such as Greyhound and Sears for a commitment of about 32% of your cash reserve. In other words, you are playing it safe with the two high-yielding stocks. These companies should have minimum downside price risk in their stocks yet reap some benefit if the interest rates do decline.

The actual buy levels of the two stocks are recorded in the appropriate column in Table 5-3. Another potential purchase for the same stocks can also be entered at 15% below the level of the initial buy. For example:

COMPANY	ACTUAL BUY LEVEL	SECOND PURCHASE AT 0.85 TIMES INITIAL BUY
Greyhound-Dial	$28	$24
Sears	34^{1}/_{2}$	29

This notation of a second purchase at the lower price allows you to consider a repeat purchase if none of your other companies falls within their buy targets. As a practical matter, if the two companies shown above did decline another 15% in price, you would probably find that many of your other monitor stocks would also be at good buy levels.

You now find yourself near the height of the stock market with a 30% commitment to a couple stocks and approximately 70% in a money market fund. The toughest thing you will now face is the urge to commit part of that 70% cash reserve for the purchase of more stocks at this high market level. You should fight that urge, even though some of your preset targets are close to a buy level. There is nothing shabby about earning 7% to 8% interest on that cash reserve in that period of time. This investment technique requires you to apply some extra patience at the high valuation levels of the stock market.

I suggest that you initiate a running tabulation of the weekly trend in the stock prices of the companies on your monitor list. This tabulation can take the form shown in Table 5-4 in the Appendix. I prefer to use the stock prices of the Friday market close. Note that I also use this tabulation to keep a running record of any transactions made during the week, such as shown in the Greyhound and Sears blocks. The time period shown in Table 5-4 includes the Iraqi invasion of Kuwait. This period is keyed to the discussion of stock transactions in this chapter, and Table 5-4 is an illustration of how you would proceed with this type of record keeping.

It was unfortunate, as shown in the tabulation, that your first transactions occurred just prior to a market decline. But that happens sometimes, and you just have to become a little more cautious with your initial cash reserve. As I show later in the text, the use of open orders did allow the Ford and James River stock to be purchased in August 1990. The mid-period of 1990 is discussed further in Chapter 8, to show how you might proceed if you were already well-entrenched in a pension plan during a severe decline of the market.

The advantage of using the Friday closing price of stocks is that it allows you to use the week-end to tabulate your stocks and to review the status of the market. The commitment of time should be minimal in this procedure, but it still allows you to maintain both a mental and recorded picture of the action of the stocks in your monitor list versus the movement of the market.

Of course, you may follow the activity of your stocks on a daily basis, but this generally involves observing the prices from newspaper tables. You might even make a decision for a purchase at any time during the week if a substantial break occurs in the prices of your stocks.

Another tabulation I suggest you maintain is a running list of your actual stock transactions as shown in Table 5-5. This type of permanent record is especially useful in a taxable account but it is also deemed important for the pension portfolio to help keep track of your transaction dates and stock costs.

Learn to apply a little flexibility within these buy guidelines. You may have noted that the original buy targets in Table 5-3 were rounded off to the nearest dollar. Don't worry about that last 1/4 point on your purchase, but rather, whether the stock you are interested in is near the reasonable range you have targeted.

NUMBER OF SHARES USED IN TRANSACTION

The number of shares of stock that you choose to use for each transaction can be considered an integral part of this technique. I suggested 100 share blocks for the initial purchases. That size block of shares was predicated on starting out with a $20,000 cash base, and even this limits your diversification somewhat, especially if you purchase the higher priced stocks.

However, there is nothing wrong during your early investing program for you to purchase less then the 100 share blocks, which are called round lots. The smaller sized purchases, called odd-lots, incur a slight premium on your transaction commission, but the benefits of the greater diversification would be worth the added cost. I would further suggest that you standardize on at least 50 shares per transaction if you begin to trade in odd-lots. Since there is usually a minimum commission charged for each stock transaction, smaller amounts of shares can increase the percentage cost of the trade. I am satisfied that the 100 share round lots are practical in a retirement plan with up to a level of $300,000 in assets. There will come a time when you will shift into 200 shares or more for most of your block transactions as your portfolio grows in size. You will probably do this on a gradual basis depending on the type and number of companies that you include in your portfolio.

Regardless of the number of shares you use at any stage of your program, I suggest you think in terms of equal lots. For example, if you are at the 100 share level, keep your transactions of all the individual companies at 100 shares, and even buy repeat blocks of the same company at that same lot level. This concept just appears to give you a safer road to travel. If you buy 100 shares each of a $10 stock and a $20 stock and anticipate a 30% gain before you sell, then you are really looking for a before-commission gain of $300 for the lower priced stock versus $600 for the original $20 stock. Sure, you made $300 more on the $20 stock, but you also had twice as much of your assets committed to the higher priced security. This technique makes each transaction achieve its own satisfactory percentage gain and lets the overall gain of all your transactions be a measure of your eventual success.

The philosophy of equal block purchases is especially important when you leverage your investment in certain companies as their stocks decline in price. For example, it is safer to buy a second equal block if a specific stock price has dropped from $20 to $10 than to buy twice as many shares at the lower level. You have, in effect, limited your upside profit potential, but you have also reduced any potential loss. The benefit of this type of thinking will be apparent as you continue to use this conservative technique.

However, even though you will find that the purchase of equal blocks of shares will work for most periods of times, I also suggest some flexibility in your thinking at other times. For example, if you were to purchase 200 share blocks at some point, and your cash reserve was diminished, it might be prudent to make some additional purchases at the 100 share level. Conversely, if you were in a 100 share mode of investing and found yourself with ample cash after a severe decline in the market, it might then be advantageous to buy some larger blocks of stock of your specific companies.

When to Sell Stocks

There are a number of guidelines that can help you determine the best sell price of a stock after it has been purchased. It is almost impossible to give you a simple formula, or a fixed percentage, to employ for all situations. Certainly the knowledge of the yearly price range of a particular stock can provide you a good starting point, but more important will be the knowledge that you will eventually gain from staying with the same companies long term.

The point at where you might consider it advantageous to sell is primarily based on achieving a reasonable percentage gain over your original purchase price. I suggest that you consider a gross profit of 30% as a goal for your initial transactions. This goal will not provide frequent trades in the beginning, and that will allow you a little time to get familiar with your stocks. A purchase of a stock at a $20 level, for example, would then provide a sell at $26 for the 30% gain.

The actual percentage gains targeted will vary both in magnitude and between the stocks as your portfolio grows in size and you become more familiar with your group of stocks. A percentage gain that you might seek for your transaction can also depend on your cash reserve level or the level of the DJIA. Say that you have initially marked a 30% gain for a stock after it was purchased. As you reduce your cash reserve because of additional purchases, you might want to drop the sell level of some of your stocks for a potential gain of 20% so that you can begin to replenish your cash reserve.

When the DJIA level is high, you should settle for lower percentage gains in your transactions, and conversely, you should reach for higher gains when the Dow level is near its low for the year. The overall object of this technique is to keep generating a satisfactory growth in your money base so that your trading leverage improves with each cycle of the market. I suggest that you use pencil notations in the sell column of your Table 5-3 tabulation so that you can make adjustments as the market conditions change.

The higher you set your net gain from a transaction, the less frequently you will incur a trading commission. However, do not make the payment of a commission a prime factor in whether or not you make a transaction. The longer the stock is held in your portfolio, the more you will want the higher gain in your transaction. For example, you might settle for a 15% gain for a particular stock within a period of a month, but may reach for a 30% gain as the holding period of the stock approaches a year in duration.

The fact that you are dealing with a pension portfolio of conservative companies allows you to work with smaller profit margins per trade because you do not have the tax consequences to immediately consider. You should acquire the confidence that the steady growth of your asset base can often come from selling stocks for small gains.

For this technique to be successful, you must set a sell target for every stock you purchase. I suggested earlier that you first employ about 30% profit goals. The initial buys of Greyhound and Sears in the sample portfolio would then show the following mental sell targets in the appropriate column of the Table 5-3 tabulation.

	PURCHASE PRICE	MENTAL SELL TARGET
Greyhound	$28	$36
Sears	34^{1}/_{2}$	$45

You may observe that the prices for the mental sells are recorded at the nearest round number. That is just a goal at this point because the actual sell price can be implemented at any deviation from the recorded figure.

How to Use Open Orders

The stock transactions in your pension portfolio are usually made through your broker at the best market price prevailing at that time. This is the most common way to make a transaction during stock market conditions where stock prices tend to move in some relatively slow up or down trend.

The use of open orders, however, might be a useful tool for you during periods of time when you cannot keep daily track of the market, or when the market becomes chaotic in either the up or down direction. In these cases, you can provide your broker with a designated buy or sell order that might vary 10 to 15% from the current price level of the stock. This method allows you to reach for a stock price that you anticipate might occur within a matter of hours or days from a condition of panic selling or buying pressure in the market at the moment.

A number of different steps can be employed with these open orders that are used primarily on the NYSE and ASE:

1. The open order can be placed on a one-day basis, which automatically cancels the order if it is not consummated by the close of the market on that specified day at your specified price.

2. The open order can also be entered "good until canceled." You will receive a written confirmation for the order that is placed beyond the one-day stipulation.

3. Even though the NYSE and ASE do not presently accept open orders placed for a week or month, your broker might agree to monitor your stocks, for short time periods, and initiate a buy or sell order on your specific instructions.

4. How open orders are used in the NASDAQ market will often depend on the brokerage firm. Some firms may only accept a

day order, some for only a week. You will have to check this out on an individual basis.

5.   Keep a running record of open orders by a type of tabulation as shown in Table 5-6 of the Appendix. You always have to be aware of your cash reserve relative to your open orders so that your cash base is ample to cover the outstanding orders.

6.   The open order should not be specified in round numbers, but rather should be placed for an advantageous position into the records of the specialist. For example, if you wanted to buy a stock at approximately \$20 in a declining market, you should place the open order at $1/_8$ point above the round number and stipulate a \$20$1/_8$ buy level. Conversely, if you wanted to sell a stock in a rising market, you would issue an open sell order at $1/_8$ point below the round number or \$19$7/_8$ in the case of the \$20 stock level.

7.   If you place an open order, and it is not triggered during the time period you had anticipated, take another look at the situation and make a judgement whether you want to continue the order, adjust its level, or just cancel it.

Let's consider how you might use an open order for the initial transaction of Sears in your sample portfolio. You bought 100 shares at \$34$1/_2$ and are mentally geared to sell that position at \$45 for a gross gain of approximately 30%. Consider that the Federal Reserve set in motion a downward bias in interest rates and the stock market takes off with a strong upward move. It is possible that the price of the Sears stock could move up to \$43 in a matter of days, just under your target sell point of \$45.

At this point, a prudent decision would be to place an open order for $47^7/$_8$ and take your chances of getting it sold at that price. If the market stabilized and the Sears stock only rose to the $47 level, it would then be a pretty good idea to sell at this established price and cancel the open order. In other words, you did not achieve the extra profit you were hoping for, but the actual sell price still produced another 4% gain over that of your original mental sell level of $45.

The stock market might instead take a strong downward move if higher interest rates occurred right after you made your initial purchases. You now have about $13,000 left in your money market fund and are in a position to commit more money for the purchase of stocks. Both Greyhound and Sears, in your sample portfolio, will have probably declined in price so they are left in a holding pattern.

It is now prudent to use open orders to buy stocks at even lower prices than you had earlier expected. Pick a few companies out of your monitor list, other than from the consumer area, and place an open buy order at a substantial discount to your original targets. Never forget that you had started your portfolio near the market top so that some downside risk is always present.

A number of companies that would have fit this scenario in mid-1990 were Ford, General Cinema, James River, LaFarge, or Witco. All of these companies were not too far from their two year average low price. But during a rapidly declining stock market, you would hesitate to make a purchase at your original preset target, but you should rather consider a price about 15% below it. These open buy orders placed "good until canceled" might look like this:

COMPANY	ORIGINAL BUY PRESET TARGET	OPEN BUY ORDERS
Ford	$44	37^{1}/_{8}$
General Cinema	21	18$^{1}/_{8}$
James River	26	22$^{1}/_{8}$
LaFarge	15	13$^{1}/_{8}$
Witco	36	30$^{1}/_{8}$

It is unlikely that all of these open orders would trigger at the same time during any rapid decline in the market. You could still make a request with your broker that as soon as any two of those open buy orders are fulfilled, the broker is authorized to cancel the remaining orders. Re-evaluate the stock prices again at this point and consider the placement of several new open orders based on the current status of the market.

For example, consider that both Ford and James River were bought at 37^{1}/_{8}$ and 22^{1}/_{8}$ respectively. Another $6,000 was used from your cash reserve for these purchases and you now have about $7,700 left from your original cash commitment. You could sit tight with the four stocks and $7,700, but you could also consider committing another 50% of your remaining cash. This can be done by placing new open orders at about 15% below the prices you used during the first open buy procedure, as shown below.

COMPANY	ORIGINAL PRESET BUY	FIRST OPEN BUY ORDER	NEW OPEN BUY ORDER
General Cin.	$21	18^{1}/_{8}$	15^{3}/_{8}$
LaFarge	15	13$^{1}/_{8}$	11$^{1}/_{8}$
Witco	36	30$^{1}/_{8}$	25$^{1}/_{8}$

If any two of the above orders are fulfilled, then the other orders are immediately canceled and the portfolio stands pat at that time. You now have six companies in your portfolio and will have to patiently wait the price action of the stocks. Your next transaction should be a sell order for a designated percentage gain for at least one of the stocks in your portfolio.

The use of open orders will initially feel awkward to you. As I mentioned earlier, you would not generally utilize the open order if you can easily monitor the market, or if the stock prices are moving in slow, normal trends. Open orders are especially useful when repeat transactions are made in the same company, but these multiple purchases are only suggested after you have initially diversified into a few companies.

These simple guidelines should help you get a start with a relatively small pension portfolio. As the portfolio grows in value, you will find yourself with more flexibility and better able to apply the benefits of the open order.

How to Use the Technique at Market Lows

Remember that you are basically going to buy shares at the most recent two year low price range of the stock. This technique gives your portfolio some downside price protection during any major drop in the market. But that still does not mean that these conservative stocks could not lose another 10% to 40% of their value during a severe slump in the market.

I know that it is easy for me to talk about additional asset losses in your portfolio while you may be distraught at the very idea. But you must develop the confidence that these periods have occurred many times in the past history of the stock market.

You should learn to enjoy investing at these low stock prices in anticipation of eventual greater profits during the market recovery. Of course, you are not going to enjoy anything unless you had maintained a sizable cash reserve in your portfolio prior to the decline of the market. Go ahead and start your further stock buys, utilizing the procedure of open orders whenever possible.

This can be considered Dollar Cost Averaging at its best. You should count on almost being out of cash in your pension portfolio at the extreme lows of the market. And if your account receives additional cash deposits during this period, consider the purchase of more shares. This strategy is suited for the years prior to retirement. The minimum cash level of 20% always appears prudent to maintain during your retirement years.

At least one of your portfolio companies will probably have its stock price rise during these low market periods. Whether you let the rise in the price continue or sell and transfer the proceeds into another stock is a judgement call. You should try to maintain a nearly full invested position with as many shares as you can accumulate, but at some point, cash must be raised in your portfolio.

How to Use the Technique as Market Rises Substantially

The major upward moves of the stock market from depressed levels that might occur about four to ten times over the next twenty years, should help produce good gains in the asset base of your portfolio. You should tend to reach for higher sell levels in your stocks as the stock market rebounds from a very low point. In other words, you should resist raising cash in a fast manner.

Why should you raise cash at all on a significant upswing of the market? Because nobody really knows how high, or for how long, a market trend will last. Therefore, the act of building up a cash reserve by taking profits in your stock positions is the conservative bent of this recommended investment technique. After all, the cash reserve eventually is how you will be able to make new stock purchases during any fall-back in the market.

Variable percentage gains should be considered for your sell transactions as the market recovers from an extreme low. You should think in terms of 40% to 50% profits for your first sell transactions. Further gains from sell transactions might be in the 30% zone, as the market averages return to about 80% to 90% of the last high of the market. As the DJIA reaches and surpasses the previous high point, I would begin to think in terms of smaller 10% to 20% profit gains between the purchase and sell transactions of the same stock. You will probably find yourself in an irregular process of building up your cash reserve during this upward move of the stock market.

When to Stop Raising Cash

I believe that one of your tough decisions will be to determine at what point to stop raising cash during any strong upward move of stock prices in the market. Some investment advisors might exit the stock market completely at a high valuation in the market. I still work on the theory that no one knows for sure where a market top will occur in any one given cycle. I recommend that you raise your cash position back to the 50% level of your portfolio value, and then sit back for awhile and enjoy any further price appreciation of your stocks. What a spot to be in; you have made some money, you now have available investment cash, you have stocks that can still grow in price, and you can sleep contently.

At some point, depending on various economic signs or world events, your gut feeling might tell you to take further stock profits and increase the percentage of your cash position. Use a step-by-step approach by spreading your transactions over a period of time. Even then, I suggest that your cash position should not be greater then 70% to 80% of your portfolio assets. You should consider selling the stocks in your portfolio that have appreciated the most in price.

Let me elaborate a little more on this situation because each person's gut feeling may be quite different. In fact, I am not sure what my reaction will be, since I have never experienced a time yet when I wanted to raise cash much above the 50% level of the pension portfolio. I do not believe you can rely on the market averages alone as a guide because if the DJIA continues to reach new highs, you will find yourself automatically selling off some more of your stocks that are also reaching new highs. Like it or not, you are almost forced to do this in a disciplined manner so that your cash ratio does not drop much below the 50% level at these times.

However, I believe I would get edgy at some point, if all the conservative stocks on my monitored list appear to be trading at PE ratios much higher than historical valuations. That might be seen with PE number above the 30 level. And, if maybe 90% of the stock market advisors and analysts were still predicting further market appreciation at this time, that would really make me nervous. It should take some significant data before you consider a drastic rise in the cash percentage of your portfolio much over the 50% level.

Regardless of where your high cash zone stabilizes, you are now in a desirable position to be able to buy certain stocks again as their prices drop at least 15% to 20% below the levels of your last sell transactions. This can be considered the basic starting point of your next trading cycle. Of course, a trading cycle in the stock market can really initiate at any stock to cash ratio point in your portfolio. It still always comes down to whether you can purchase and sell stocks at the right price.

Repeat Transaction of the Same Stock

At some point, you will probably find yourself considering the purchase of additional stock in a company in which you had already taken a position. In fact, this step is often desirable when applied to good companies drawn from the cyclical groups whose stock prices have been depressed in the marketplace. I earlier suggested that you employ a second buy target about 15% below your original purchase for the same number of shares as acquired in your original purchase. One caution sign before you double up on a particular stock might be if its price is trending downward while the overall market is heading up.

If you do double up on a specific stock, the sell target in your tabulation can then be modified to be able to quickly regain a satisfactory cash position. This can be accomplished by setting a lower anticipated price gain for the sale of the repeat purchase. You could still settle for the higher percentage target that you had earlier set on the original stock purchase, but that would be at your discretion. It can be considered a good conservative approach when smaller percentage gains are taken on stock transactions whenever these profits occur during short periods of time.

An example of a repeat transaction can be illustrated with the original purchase of 100 shares of Sears at a price of 34\frac{1}{2}$ in your portfolio. The potential sell target for a 30% gain would require a price of $45 for Sears to occur before the stock is sold. Instead, consider that the price of Sears stock actually declined to $29 during a drop in the market. Consider that another purchase of Sears was made and a new sell target for only a 20% gain or $35 can be placed on this second block of 100 shares. If your original purchase was also adjusted for a 20% gain, then the new sell target price would be shown as $41 instead of the original notation of $45.

You will learn to experiment over the years when you begin to buy and then subsequently sell repetitive blocks of shares of the same company. I do not want to infer that your program should deviate from the fundamental concepts expressed earlier, but there are always subtle ways you can change your trading procedures. One method I sometimes have used when I average down in well-known company is to sell the last block of stock purchased at the level of the cost of the preceding purchase. An example of this method is shown below:

As Stock Price Falls
Purchase Of Block A at $40 per share
Buy Block B at $34
Buy Block C at $29
Buy Block D at $25

As Stock Price Rises
Sell The Last Block D at $29 per share
Sell The Block C at $34
Sell The Block B at $40
Sell the Block A at some desired % gain over cost

That information shows that the repeat purchases are made in fixed steps of about 15% after the initial stock position is taken. I might use this procedure more at market tops when I want to keep generating cash into the portfolio. Another variation of that procedure can occur when you do not want to commit too much cash too fast. In this case, you can keep increasing the percentages of the steps between consecutive purchases. For example:

As Stock Price Falls
Purchase first Block A
Buy Block B at 15% below cost of Block A
Buy Block C at 20% below cost of Block B
Buy Block D at 25% below cost of Block C

How to Arrive at a Fair Return

This technique proposes that you think consistently in terms of relatively small percentage gains on the trades of the large, mature companies in your stock portfolio. Investors sometimes will roll-over certificates of deposit based on differences of only $1/_2$% in the interest rates. It is easy to understand how the gain in income is obtained by this sort of trading method when it refers to CD's. Unfortunately, the net return of this type of investment leaves little real growth left after the inflation rate is considered.

If you now expend energy in looking for $1/_2$% to 1% differences in interest rates for your investments, why not use some of that energy looking for better ways to achieve a greater income? This only requires you to gain confidence in the use of large, mature companies as a cornerstone of a conservative technique for stock trading. Learn to add up the different ways that your stock investments can make your assets grow in your portfolio over the longer period of time.

One prime way to help you achieve success with stocks is to consider that the dividend yield is always part of your total investment return. While the pay-out of a dividend may not enter into an investment decision for the smaller growth company, it does play a significant role with the large, mature companies. This is your way to obtain those few extra percentage points on your overall portfolio.

Conversely, several of the lower yielding stocks in your portfolio might show higher price volatility during any given year. This condition might allow you to employ a little more trading activity without the need to count on receiving a dividend. Learn to use both methods in a pension portfolio so that your annual total return oscillates at levels at least 6% to 8% above the return of a CD.

For example, consider that you had earlier bought the Sears stock for 34\frac{1}{2}$ with a yield of about 6% and your total in-and-out brokerage commission cost was 3%. You could then sell that block of Sears after one year at a price of 38\frac{1}{2}$, which returns a 12% gain on the trade. The total return for that transaction actually results in a 15% increase if you consider the dividend received minus the commission. On the other hand, a stock with a low yield must return a greater price change in order to reach a satisfactory net return for the year.

You can also consider working on even smaller price mark-ups and trade the same block of shares a couple times within the year. This is especially apt to occur in a relatively stagnant market, during which the DJIA may only drift within a 200 point range. For example, a stock like Baxter may vary $3 to $4 in stock price several times during a given year. Disregard the low dividend yield and just consider the gain on the transaction. Buying Baxter at $20 and selling at $23 would give you a gross gain of 15% minus the 3% commission for a net of 12%.

If you can repeat this transaction for Baxter at least one more time within a stagnant market year, its effect on your portfolio would be significant. Any interest that might accrue in your money market fund from the proceeds of the original sell would tend to add another 1% to 3% to your overall gain. You also may be fortunate to receive a dividend during the period of time you held the stock, which provides an additional bonus.

This procedure, if repeated for a couple of your stocks during relatively quiet periods of the market, can provide additional growth for the assets in your portfolio. Do not worry about how much the broker is earning. At times, the broker might come out of the trade with 10% to 30% of your net earnings. So be it!

CHAPTER 6: THE TECHNIQUE FURTHER EXPLORED

Since the road to investment success is often paved with confusing signs, I want to enlarge on some of the key concepts of the recommended technique to provide additional confidence.

TRADING VERSUS BUY AND HOLD

You may question whether the strategy of holding stocks for many years (Buy and Hold) in a portfolio will out-perform a trading technique. Of course, it could happen, but the odds would be against you during recent years. You have to be very adept at picking the right stocks, and that has become ever more difficult in this rapidly changing world. Even professional management groups have to continually buy and sell stocks in today's market in order to beat the average returns.

One problem with buying and holding a portfolio of stocks for long-term appreciation is that you would need to diversify into companies with a higher rate of growth, and that generally means lower yields from dividends. It is easier to pick the well-known, mature companies and trade their routine price cycles while collecting good dividends. But there is nothing wrong with combining the two techniques if that makes you feel comfortable. Remember, it is the bottom line that counts and there is no rule against being flexible in your investments if that works out for you. For example, you could trade one half of your portfolio and keep the other half of your portfolio in long-term growth stocks.

The trading procedures that were outlined earlier should not be construed as a rapid turnover technique, although it is conceivable that some transactions could occur in a matter of weeks. Other stock positions might be

101

maintained for a period of a couple years awaiting some appreciable move in their prices. In time, some stocks will be deemed to be better suited for the trading of price variations than others. The selection of new stocks for your portfolio is part of a slow evolution process of this conservative technique of trading.

STOCKS CHOSEN FOR BUY AND HOLD

I try to resist thinking of stocks in terms of Buy and Hold because I believe the stock of any company should be considered for sale at some point in time. If Buy and Hold does have a place in stock investments, it is probably better applied to the newer companies that have a potentially successful future in a growth industry. In these cases, you would be looking for a rising revenue pattern of a company which should show up in earnings growth. This growth should be eventually reflected in the price of the shares of its stock.

Companies that grow rapidly usually start out from a lower capitalization base and have developed a new product that can stand out in a competitive economy. It is likely that some of these companies will split their stocks over a period of time to increase their participation in the stock market. Therefore, if you were lucky enough to hold the stock one of these companies over a period of years, the return on your investment could be much greater than what may be achieved by the conservative trading method that I recommend. But it is much more of a gamble to look out years in advance for these smaller companies. If you happen to gain confidence in a company of this type, you might want to include its stock in a personal, taxable portfolio rather than the tax-deferred pension plan.

There are other large, well-established companies that could also be candidates for the Buy and Hold strategy over long periods of time. These companies participate significantly in the economy with their products and benefit from the world-wide population growth. They will generally be less affected by economic cycles than the other companies that are shown to be better suited for trading purposes.

I consider companies such as General Electric, Procter & Gamble, and Dow Chemical to fit into this growth category of investment grade stocks. That does not mean that their stocks will not rise or fall in price during any given year, but normally, their yield and growth patterns are fairly safe. Another way to do it, if you are more comfortable with a Buy and Hold strategy is to pick the biggest and best-run companies you can locate. These investment-grade companies tend to have their stock decline less in falling markets, while their stock prices recover well when the economy recovers. These stocks also tend to provide the core holdings of most conservative individual investors as well as the pension institutions.

HOW TO LOOK AT PRICE TRENDS IN STOCKS

Buying and selling stocks is only complex if you make it so. The humorist Will Rodgers, many years ago, suggested "that you should only buy stocks that go up – and if the stocks don't go up in price – don't buy them." That bit of humor offers a simple guideline that is easy to understand, but the advice may not prove useful to you in a practical sense.

I will attempt to weave a simple practical guideline around the idea that the stock prices of many of the financially sound companies have to go down before they can go back up in price. Therefore, why not buy these stocks when their prices are down? This guideline does not have humor to it, but it does have the best chance to do what Will Rodgers specified for success. I believe all you require are a few guidelines so you can feel comfortable with the rising and falling trends of stock prices.

One key point that has been previously expressed is that the stock price of most mature companies will rise and fall within a period of a year by a significant amount. I do not want to infer that the high and low price levels will always return to the same point during these cycles. That would be desirable with the use of a trading technique, but nothing is that simple in the stock market.

Sometimes during a given year, the high will be higher than the previous year's high, and the low's of the stock will also stay above the previous year's low. This pattern generally occurs in a broad, upward trend of the stock market. Conversely, in a declining stock market that could extend over a couple of years, the outer limits of the range usually drift downward. This trend should be considered over a period of years for each of the stocks you are following in your monitor list. The past history of the price ranges of the companies are available from either the financial services or the annual reports of the individual companies.

The stock price of a typical large, mature company might show the following pattern in a rising economy.

YEARLY PRICE RANGE

YEAR	HIGH	LOW
1	$35	$20
2	41	24
3	44	27
4	40	25

Let's look at how you may pursue a trading program during the four year period for this stock. If you observe that the stock price drifted down from $35 to $22 in the first year, you might just make your first purchase at that level. A profit target set at 40% would mean that you anticipate to sell off that specific block of stock at about $31. After that sale was consummated, your weekly monitor list would show that the stock price kept rising in value until a level of $41 was reached in the second year. In effect, you lost $10 of additional appreciation by selling early, but that was only seen in hindsight.

You will note that the stock price drifts back down to the lower levels, but you would have to surmise that the low of $20 for year 1 will not be reached in year 2. A reasonable price target for another purchase could then be placed at 20% below the original sale price of $31, or about $25. If this purchase occurs at the $25 level, and you are still seeking a 40% gain, then the potential sale of this new block of stock would be about $35.

In this particular scenario, as soon as you sell, you again note that the stock keeps rising in price so that it eventually tops out at $44 during the third year of your program. I know it is tough to sit back and observe that you sold too early, but that is how this technique functions. On the other hand, the trading technique balances out over the years because you will often sell a position near its high price for that particular cycle.

After that last sale at $35, you continue to monitor the stock and hope that you will make another purchase if the stock drops back to about 20% below the $35 level. That means a new target of about $28 is set for the next possible purchase. You can deduce from this procedure that you are riding an upward trend which may last for several years.

Let's say you actually bought another block of shares at the $28 level and target another 40% gain. This would anticipate a sale of $39. After this sale occurs in the fourth year, you could be surprised to see that only a high of $40 is reached before the stock price starts drifting down again. So the disappointment you might have felt during the previous year because of the premature sale is now replaced with the good feeling that comes from getting out of a stock position near its high price for the year.

As you gain confidence and experience with this technique you might decide to hold off the purchase of a new block of stock for this particular company because the high price reached in the fourth year was actually below that of the preceding year. You should always be alert to this change of the price pattern in the stock of the large, mature companies. So instead of buying at about $31, which would represent a 20% reduction from the last sale of $39, you might wait to see at what area the stock price tends to stabilize. This stabilization might take as long as a year to occur. You then observe that the low price of $25 is eventually reached, and if your cash position is sufficient, you might start another investment cycle in this particular stock.

Consider that you first bought this stock in the first year at $22 and held it throughout the four year period. Your shares are now worth $25 at the low point of its price range which only gave you a $3 gain or about 14% over the four year period. On the other hand, you did pretty well if you had bought at $22 and sold out at the $40 high during the fourth year, but not as well as if you had traded every year. Moreover, the mechanical buy and sell steps are actually easier to apply in practice. It tends to be quite difficult for most persons to make a major decision for a stock transaction at some high or low price level of a particular stock.

As I mentioned in earlier chapters, the types of companies you would like to accumulate in a monitor list will generally have more than one cycle of reasonable price variations within the duration of a year. If you traded for relatively reasonable profits of 15% to 20% during these cycles, the net gain in your portfolio would certainly surpass the Buy and Hold approach for these same companies. Remember that I am discussing the tax-deferred portfolio where trading commissions are your basic costs.

The upward trend of a growth company could be strong enough so that the low price of its stock during one year is in close proximity to the high price of its stock of the previous year. It then becomes difficult to trade repeatedly in this type of stock during any given year. Obviously, these types of stock patterns would produce much better profits if the companies are held in the portfolio for substantial periods of time. An example of this pattern might show:

YEARLY PRICE RANGE

YEAR	HIGH	LOW
1	$35	$20
2	51	33
3	63	47
4	75	60

PROTECTING YOUR PROFITS

You can protect a substantial portion of the appreciation in the price of your stocks by the use of a stop-loss order. Unfortunately, this protective order is accepted only for the listed issues of the NYSE and ASE markets. The O-T-C stocks do not have a mechanism for the stop-loss order, although it is possible that your broker might provide some sell protection based on your instructions.

The stop-loss order is placed with your broker and stipulates that in the event of a decline in the price of your stock, your stock (or some part of it) should be sold at the level that you designate. These orders are usually placed 10% to 15% below the currently quoted price of the of the stocks you hold, but they are less practical for the types of companies that I recommend for the pension portfolio. For example, if you purchased a specific conservative stock for $30 and planned to sell it at $39 for a 30% profit, there is little value in placing a 10% stop-loss order after the stock price reaches, say, the $36 level. On any dip in the market, the 10% stop order will sell out your stock position at a price of $32^1/$_2$, which would provide you a minimal profit on your transaction. The sad part of this scenario is that the stock price may drift back up to the $36 level, and you found yourself out of the position.

As you proceed with this trading technique, you will continue to gain confidence and flexibility in how to handle stock trades for reasonable profits. You will find that it is not always the use of fixed profit steps that will produce the ultimate results. You will have to develop a mental attitude that will eventually lead you to take different profits at different times. After all, it's the sum total of the big profits, small profits, and even the occasional loss over a period of time that will determine whether you have really achieved investment success in your program. The discipline that you will acquire will lead you to take profits at an appropriate market opportunity within the framework of your portfolio.

For example, if you buy a stock at $30 and watch it rise to a price of $36 it might be wise to just sell it at that time for a 20% gain even though you were originally hoping for a 30% profit. This premature sell might occur if additional cash is needed in the portfolio, or if you deem the market to be uncertain at that period of time. A reasonable profit of 20% would always be prudent if the ratio of the stock to cash position is relatively high in your portfolio. And working on a close profit of 20% in a stock transaction will generally preclude the use of the stop-loss order.

On the other hand, if you do hold some growth stocks long term and hope to double or triple your original purchase price, then the use of the stop-loss order can be a desirable procedure. For example, consider that you had bought a stock for $22 per share and watched its price rise to $51. A 15% stop-loss order could be placed at $43, which would still give you a 100% gain on your purchase if some event suddenly occurred to rapidly drop the price of the stock. You must acquire the mental attitude that it is beneficial to sell in this case for a 100% profit than to watch the stock price continue to decline.

The fact that you lost $8 per share in profit (from the $51 to the $43 level) must be quickly dismissed from your mind since this is how the stock market functions sometime. This stock could continue to drift down in price to the $33 level, at which time you might buy another block because you still like its future outlook. Your mental attitude should benefit from the fact that you now have the same block of stock in a company from which you had earlier pocketed $21 per share of profit (the difference between the $43 sale and the $22 original purchase). The new stock position at the $33 purchase will now have to stand on its own merits.

However, let's say the purchase at $33 was a poor decision and the price of the stock continues to drift down toward the original $22 level. You still have come out ahead on the overall set of trades. You have, of course, lost $11 in paper value (from $33 to $22), but when compared to the profit of $21 you received from the earlier sale, you still find yourself in the plus column.

The protective stop-loss order could have also been applied in the above scenario if you had bought back into the stock at $33. While it was a reasonable price, you were uncertain about the underlying reasons that caused the stock to drift down from the $51 price. In this case, a stop-loss order placed at 15% below $33 would take you out of the stock position at the $28 level. This additional loss of $5 now leaves you with only a $16 profit less the commissions from your original investment. But you now have the cash from the stop sale returned to your portfolio for further investment activity. This is certainly better than sitting with the paper loss in the stock as it continued its decline to the $22 level.

You may observe that the stock price appears to stabilize at the $22 level and the company is now poised to take advantage of a recovery in the economy. You could then proceed to take another stock position at this lower price level to initiate a new cycle of investment in the company. The whole price cycle for certain large growth companies might take a couple years to complete, and it will generally take a significant contraction in the economy for it to occur in the first place.

I do not specifically recommend that you pursue the use of the stop-loss procedures routinely, but you should be aware of how it can be applied as shown in the above example. The object of a successful investor is to learn every protective procedure you can over the years. It should be clear to you that the Buy and Hold method can easily shift into a long-term trading technique if you do use the stop-loss order.

The stop-loss order can also be modified upward if the stock price that you are protecting continues its rise in value. If the stock in the initial example continued its rise from $51 to $61, a new stop-loss order could then be placed at $52 to maintain the 15% differential between its current price and the price you are hoping to receive during any unforseen decline in the stock.

The use of the stop-loss order does have one disadvantage in a stock market driven down by panic selling. It is possible that the price you have specified in your order cannot be executed and you might be sold out at a market order below the price you had expected. This situation does not occur as a rule, but if it does you may still appreciate getting out of the stock position even at the reduced profit. I say profit because you would not normally place a stop-loss order for the original purchase of the type of stocks you are accumulating in your pension plan. Do not forget that the stocks of these mature companies should be first bought near their recent low price levels. However, you might still consider the use of the stop-loss order on the initial purchase of a speculative stock that you may include in your non-pension portfolio.

THE NUMBER OF STOCKS CHOSEN

I made a strong point earlier in that the diversification of a stock portfolio should provide some safety and comfort to you, both from the number and types of companies held. After all, the large number of companies held in an equity mutual fund becomes its primary selling point to the investing public. And I suggested that a portfolio of about 10 companies provides an upper practical number for an individual to handle in a self-directed pension plan.

The goal of ten companies in your program is still valid, but that should not be considered a magic number. Remember that you could have six companies in your plan and have as ample diversification because of their various divisions as you might have with ten other types of companies.

Another reason for you to diversify into different industry groups in a portfolio is that you are hopeful that the cash raised from one transaction can be effectively shifted into the stock of a company from another industry group. This new group may be adversely affected by a decline of its business activity. The use of this type of trading technique appears to have become even more effective in recent years as various industry groups keep going in and out of favor with the investment public.

It sure would be nice to retain the same raft of companies in your portfolio for years on end, but this is often difficult to achieve. As a practical matter, you will probably find that about 10 to 15 stocks will remain long-term in your monitor list of 20 companies, while others float into and out of consideration.

Out of your long-term core group, you might further find that only about 6 to 8 of these companies will exhibit the excellent price variability that is needed for the success of your program. This often means that most of the desirable trading profits, during any given year, might only come from a relatively small portion of your portfolio. Remember the key point – it is the overall return on your investment that counts.

Those stocks that drift out of the monitored list do so for a variety of reasons. They must have had some good qualities if they were chosen in the first place. Therefore, I suggest that you might even keep a second monitor list of those companies, as well as others that show some price action you like. You would only have to record their closing stock price each Friday, as you already do with your prime list of 20 companies. This procedure takes little additional time, yet provides an on-going farm club of replacements for the possible inclusion into your portfolio at some future time. I sometimes include a company into this auxiliary list for no other reason than to compare its price action against an existing portfolio stock from the same industry group.

You might also find that the general trading technique will be best served by shifting emphasis on the number of shares of stock held in certain companies of your portfolio. The best returns on investment often occur when more of the assets of a portfolio are concentrated in one or two companies. This is especially true when the stock market averages varies within a 5% to 10% trading range. Interesting enough, such large companies as Sears and Ford have proven to be effective holdings for this type of trading.

For example, if you decided at some point to take a 100 share position of Sears at, say, $35, you might then keep adding another 100 shares for every $2 to $3 decline in its stock price. This procedure keeps building up your share holdings in Sears for roughly every 7% reduction in the price of the stock.

You are basically dollar cost averaging down in this company and might find yourself with 400 shares if the Sears stock finally stabilizes at the $28 level. When the stock price rises, you then begin to take your profits at appropriate margins dependent on the cash reserve position in your portfolio. The last block of stock purchased could now be sold at a 20%, 30%, or even a 40% profit target, which you have judged on a personal perception of the market conditions at that period of time. I suggest that if you begin to concentrate more of your assets into fewer companies that the cash position of your portfolio stay a little more on the high side. In this case, you may not want to draw your cash reserves any lower than 30% of your total portfolio value.

At a given point in time, you could conceivably find the make-up of your portfolio to be as follows:

> 2 core companies comprising 50% of assets
> 6 other companies comprising 20% of assets
> Cash reserve comprising 30% of assets

The basic reason for this concentration in a couple of core companies, even though they are large and conservative, is that they allow you to take repetitive profits because of an optimum shift in the price patterns of their stocks.

You could trade the stock of only one company if you carry this idea of concentration to an extreme point. A popular saying years ago was to "place all your eggs in one basket - and watch the basket." I believe you could make a case for going against the general concept of diversification, but I do not recommend the single company approach for the pension plan or especially the self-directed retirement plan. Some diversification, at least more than a few companies, appears to be the safer path to take for your portfolio.

In another method that can be used for investment concentration, you could balance the price variations of one large company's stock against another in the same industry group. Two such match-ups might be seen with K-Mart versus Sears, or Ford versus General Motors. For example, instead of holding 600 shares of stock for one of these giants, you would take a 300 share position in each of the two similar companies.

CASH HOLDINGS

You may ask that if this trading technique provides a reasonable investment return, why not reduce the percentage of cash held in your portfolio so that more stocks can be purchased. I suggest that you stay with the key concept of this trading technique, that is, to play it safe and be ready to take advantage of any future declines in the prices of your stocks. You must keep your discipline intact so that you can resist the insidious temptation that makes you reach for greater trading profits and running out of cash at the wrong point in time. You should never forget that the cash reserves in your portfolio can be considered the ultimate of diversification.

You will no doubt experience some mental conflict when low interest rates reduce the income from the money market portion of your portfolio. For example, if the interest rate is 5% and 50% of your portfolio is in cash at a high valuation of the stock market, can that high cash level be justified? Yes it can, with the investment technique that I have outlined.

Always remember that you are trying to average out about a 15% annual growth in your pension portfolio. And that reasonable goal means that some portions of your portfolio may not be growing at all, if not actually declining at some point of time. So you could well accept a high cash position that grows at far less than a 15% growth rate, as long as you do not measure your investment success on a short-term basis.

If the market valuation continues to grow, then the 50% stock portion of your portfolio, based on the previous cash example, should also continue to grow. But if the stock market happens to decline 10%, what a spot for you to be in with a large cash position! The major growth of your pension portfolio is really not derived from the income of the interest bearing securities. It is based on the asset growth that comes from the reasonable trading profits from your stocks.

The stock portion of the portfolio is actually used as a generator of cash. In other words, I keep telling myself that if I sell a block of stock for a profit, I have generated a block of new cash that is now placed back into the portfolio. This new cash is now available for another purchase of stock at a more reasonable price.

You have already been given several guidelines about when the cash level of your portfolio may be considered too high or too low dependent on the market environment. In practice, you will probably find yourself working in some middle range of 25% to 40% of your portfolio assets in cash, more times than not. This range appears comfortable and you will no doubt gravitate toward it, especially when your portfolio increases in total value. I believe that if you pursue more profits per trade, as you start out with a small portfolio, you will find yourself at the lower end of that range.

You should always feel relatively worry-free with this type of pension portfolio. The percentage of cash in your portfolio now becomes a pivotal way to help you decide just how active you will be in your stock transactions.

It is interesting to note that stock transactions would continually occur if you tried to hold to a fixed percentage of cash. For example, if you stipulated that you would always maintain a 50% cash level and the market continued to climb, you will find yourself selling stocks in order to maintain that percentage. Conversely, if the market declined, you would have to start buying stocks to hold the cash level of your portfolio at 50%. You will no doubt be following this type of portfolio adjustment at various holding times. As a rule, I do not recommend that you think in terms of fixed numbers – stay loose – and learn to shift that cash percentage to your advantage.

A key point with this type of portfolio is that the downside losses in your stock values tend to be minimal. Many of the stocks you will find remaining in your portfolio during a market decline are probably trading down near their support levels or close to their price lows for the year. The stocks that did rise in price in your portfolio were sold out earlier and that is how you build up your cash reserve. Furthermore, even if you found yourself sitting with a major cash position and the stock market took off, rest assured that some of your sleeping stocks would also join the upward move in the market.

INVESTMENT STRATEGY

I have observed the uncertainty that many persons appear to develop concerning their overall investment plans. It is not a clear path for anyone – and include me in that group.

It is not what you earn in your lifetime, but how your side investments grow that will be your final measure of financial success. I will never forget the low wage steel worker I knew in the late 1950's who always bought a new car each year, sent two children through medical school, and had the nicest house in the neighborhood. He worked part-time during the depression of the 1930's, and he continually purchased the stocks of large capitalization companies throughout that period. Some of these stocks were priced under one dollar per share at times. And he kept buying and holding, buying and holding.

The above story leads to an important concept – it is advantageous to stick with a successful investment program, but even more importantly, you have to be in the right program for its time. Many individuals invest much of their pension assets into fixed income securities at too early an age. This is the wrong time and place for an income production program that is better left to your retirement years.

It is during your working years when a satisfactory growth of pension assets is required, and fixed income-bearing securities do not appear to be a good strategy to achieve this goal. Good growth in your personal taxable assets during your working years also appears best tuned toward the investment in stocks. This strategy should probably take a different tack than how you would proceed in the pension program. Moreover, if fixed income securities are used, they are better directed toward your personal funds during your retirement years.

I do not want to infer that fixed income securities, such as bonds or even treasury bills, cannot grow or fall in value over time. If you purchase existing bonds during a period of high interest rates, you would probably find their price to be below the original face value. This situation allows the new value of the bond to be equilibrated to the current interest rate. These bonds would then rise in their marketable price as interest rates decline, and this rise in bond price would reflect a profit in your portfolio. So bonds could be bought and sold for appreciation investing if you choose this approach. I have stayed away from this mode of investing for a couple reasons. It appears to have less flexibility and liquidity than common stocks, and it's historical investment results have been below that of stocks. Another reason I like the conservative stock technique for the whole life of a pension plan is that it tends to produce better results the more you use it. As you explore the trading methodology and gain more confidence, I do not see why you would give it up after you retire. This is your best chance to keep well above the rate of inflation.

MORE ASPECTS OF THE TECHNIQUE

Some concepts appear to hold more water than others and you will learn to shift some emphasis in those areas of stock investment. For example, one concept specifies that after a position is taken in a particular company's stock, another purchase of that stock can be undertaken below that of the original price. This concept is geared to the theory of the dollar cost averaging method.

However, you might very well take another stock position in a company such as Sears or Apple Computer at some price above your previous purchases. This strategy could occur as their stock prices drift in a narrow range and you find yourself with a large cash position. These types of decisions will continually arise as you proceed to sharpen your knowledge about your group of stocks.

At the same time, you should be careful that you do not begin to chase stocks as they rapidly rise in price. It is quite possible to make money on stocks this way but it is tricky to know exactly when to make the purchase. And secondly, the type of conservative stocks that are generally recommended for this pension technique does not have a large enough spread in its price range to warrant taking a chance at that time.

You will no doubt read or hear stock advisors state that the stocks with rising prices should be held while others should be sold. In other words, hold your winners and sell your losers. That advice is valid to some degree, but it appears more appropriate for use in the strategy for the taxable portfolio of stocks. As a general rule, I suggest that you refrain from getting drawn into this type of thinking for your pension portfolio. The contrarian approach, utilizing the conservative large company stocks, is more attuned to raise cash by selling winners while you wait patiently for your dormant stocks to rise in price.

If you follow the rudiments of the strategy I have recommended, you will generally own some stocks for a long period of years in your pension portfolio, like a Buy and Hold approach. The Buy and Hold strategy is often keyed to the price of your original purchase in that particular company.

Let's explore how this might occur with our old company standby- Sears, Roebuck. Your original purchase in Sears might be initiated at a price of $40 after you had observed that the stock traded at a high of $55 during the previous year. But as it could happen, the stock continued its decline to a price of $34. A second purchase is made at this price. Unfortunately, the Sears stock continues to decline in price to a level of $26, and you then purchase another block of the shares.

At some point, the Sears stock will recover so that you are able to sell off the last $26 block at a price of $36 for about a profit of 40%. Soon after you sell, the price of the Sears stock continues an upward trend and you are fortunate to sell the second block of shares at $44 for another 30% gain. So now you are left with your original purchase made at that $40 level. After the sale of the second block, the Sears stock resumes another price decline to the $35 level.

You might second guess yourself and wonder why you did not sell that original block at $44, and close out the Sears position at that time for a fairly good overall profit. Your portfolio has just taken a 20% paper loss on that block of Sears (from the $44 high to the $35 level). And to your dismay for the next couple years, Sears only trades in the $25 to $35 zone, while that original block stays pegged at a $40 cost basis in your portfolio. Of course, your current strategy should be to just go ahead and trade the Sears stock in that $25 to $35 range and enjoy the action from these profitable transactions.

I know that single original block of Sears at the $40 purchase level is going to keep gnawing at you – but hopefully, only in a sedate manner. This is where you could begin to accept the idea that the dormant position of the higher priced Sears in your portfolio is part of a successful technique, rather than being a detriment to your program. You should consider that the original block has now assumed a Buy and Hold status in your portfolio. You collect your dividends and wait for a good profit out there in some future transaction. Secondly, that original block of Sears now becomes important as a pivotal point in your portfolio.

That is the way I use it. This would be my prop to keep me going back to Sears every time its price drops much below $40, because that figure continually looks at me from my portfolio. Most of us need a prop if we are to maintain some discipline in any type of activity. So if you did not sell off that original block of the Sears stock at the $44 level, you could consider it a blessing for your program.

Another interesting aspect of the trading technique occurs when you reach the 50% cash position in your portfolio. This balance between the cash and stock portion of a portfolio should exist often during your program. This cash position basically signifies that you have found yourself in a period of uncertainty at a near-term topping of the market averages. The market may be uncertain, but you should not feel uncertain as to where you stand – a very comfortable position.

In fact, you are really in a win/win situation and you do not care which direction the stock market now takes. As I indicated earlier, you even began to secretly hope for a substantial downward move of stock prices, because that is how that large cash reserve you have accumulated will allow you to easily beat the averages.

Earlier, I stated that you should just stand pat at the 50% cash level. That's not necessarily so. For example, when the market averages are high, you could stay active by trading in a narrow price range for some of your stocks. Investors tend to become edgy at these high market points, and the result of this nervousness usually provides a good trading zone of 5% in the averages.

It would not make much sense to try to take advantage of this market condition if it only lasted for a short time. But who knows? It might last for months. So trading stocks for short-term gains of approximately 10% at the erratic market tops can promote a solid growth of your assets. To paraphrase the late Senator Everett Dirksen, "10% here and 10% there and pretty soon it adds up to real money."

The object is safety as well as growth, so you should use the 50% cash level as your pivot point as you oscillate your transaction around that comfortable 50-50 balance in your portfolio. You will probably use the open orders to a greater extent during this phase of your program.

I will also caution you to stick to the stocks in your portfolio that exhibit the most price volatility at the market tops. You would not want to sell off a block of Apple stock and place the cash into the purchase of one of your truly dormant stocks, even though it may be at the low end of its price range. In other words, some dormant stocks are more dormant than others. However it can be quite advantageous to roll any cash proceeds into most of your dormant stocks at the times of market bottoms.

Your strategy at the stock market tops might call for you to wait for another drop in the price of Apple, pick one of the other stocks at a reduced price that shows some action, or just hold the cash in your portfolio. Even though you are pivoting around the 50% cash position, your actual cash reserve at the newly reached market tops should actually shift, in a practical sense, within a 45% to 55% range relative to your stock position.

This zone for short-term trading will generally occur at the market tops when about 50% of the advisors are predicting higher stock prices, while most of the other market watchers are predicting a sharp decline in prices. A strong resumption in the movement of stock prices in either direction should make you revert to your normal trading strategy used for the major trends of the market.

There are other bits of knowledge that you will no doubt learn as you experience the wiles of the market. These will come to you as much from subtle experimentation in your trades as from any other source. You will tend to get a feel for the daily variations of the prices of certain stocks as well as their yearly trends. Time will be on your side as you pursue this technique.

CHAPTER 7: STOCK INVESTMENTS OUTSIDE OF PENSION PLANS

If you are in a position to prepare for your own retirement with tax-deferred investments, you certainly will have an interest in what to do with your other funds. Since the amount of money that you can shelter in an IRA or other retirement plans might be limited, it behooves you to make your other investment assets grow as fast as possible to help supplement your retirement income.

I still believe that the investment in common stocks offers you the best chance to attain a good return for your efforts. Even thought the investment in real estate has also been good for a number of people, that area for success appears to be less certain in recent years. The trading of the stocks of large, conservative companies may not work as well for you in a taxable account as it does for the pension plan. But there are other ways you can invest in stocks for your personal assets so that your pension portfolio of conservative stocks is well balanced.

I suggest that you use some form of stock investment program for your taxable funds because you can use many of the same techniques that you develop for the assets of your pension plan. It makes sense to me that it is better to concentrate, what little time you may have, within the tight circle of stock investments. This allows you to gain more confidence and insight with stocks within a shorter period of time.

The following sections concentrate on some investment ideas and strategies that include the use of secondary and small capitalization companies in a taxable stock portfolio. I personally feel more comfortable with the large, mature companies, but that does not mean that the smaller company cannot be utilized for successful investment. There are numerous periods of time when the stocks of smaller companies will actually appreciate in value at a much faster rate than the larger companies.

The small company stock portfolio is of interest to many investors, especially the young. And because the mutual funds that specialize in small growth companies are a viable alternative to handling your own portfolio, especially during your early years, I have also included some ideas on that investment approach.

AGE OF INVESTOR

If there is one bit of advice I can give you, it would be to start investing early in your working life. The main reason most of us have to reach for relatively high levels of investment return is that most savings programs start fairly late in our lives. It took me a long time before I fully recognized the benefits of compounding interest on a savings account. I do not believe many people comprehend its benefits even today.

The main point I am stressing is that small sums of money invested at reasonable rates of return should not be downplayed. Most young people with money to invest outside of pension contributions often want to make big gains in a short time period for a multitude of personal reasons. There is really nothing wrong with that goal except it is a most difficult one, unless you can devote a lot of time to that task. And high gain investing is better left to the middle-aged years when your financial position is better defined. The middle years are also, hopefully, those with more yearly income and that should allow some extra funds to be invested actively.

But the years 25 to 40 for most persons are the lower income years when most of your time and efforts are involved in occupation and family activities. However, it is during these very years that you can set up a more secure retirement life. Do not forget that active lifestyles are now being seen among 70 and 80 year old people. It is hard to imagine what the year 2020 will bring about in the aging process and for how long people will be able to enjoy the fruits of retirement.

That is why I stress that investing outside the tax-deferred plans should also be started early, when lower rates of return are acceptable in order to produce substantial assets in the later years. For example, a net return of 7% in 1990 could be considered easily attainable after taxes. If you only made a one-time deposit of $2,000 into an account and counted on this growth rate to be maintained over time, observe how this single deposit will have grown throughout the years.

POINT IN TIME	VALUE OF $2000 COMPOUNDED AT 7% RATE	TIME PERIOD CONSIDERED	AMOUNT EARNED IN EACH PERIOD
After 20 years	7,740	First 20 years	5,740
After 30 years	15,225	Years 20 to 30	7,485
After 40 years	29,950	Years 30 to 40	14,725
After 50 years	58,920	Years 40 to 50	28,970

And this was only for $2,000. I especially would point out that the fund grew by $28,920 between years 40 to 50. If you have started at age 22, that only means you will be at age 72 after the 50 year period of saving. Since I am actively involved with persons at this age – believe me – that is far from hanging it up. And if you wanted to use the $30,000 at age 62, that is not too bad a deal, either.

Some questions might arise in your mind that might keep you from investing in those early years. And they can always be answered by other questions. What if the money I save is not worth too much after 50 years? What if it is? And what if I die before I spend it? What if you do not? You could keep this exercise going – but get the point – do not hold off starting your retirement program.

TAX CONSEQUENCES

I have personally stayed away from tax-free investments such as municipal bonds. It always appeared to me that if you get your mind thinking about how to pay less taxes, you lose a step in investing for bigger returns. Why not invest for the 15% returns and gladly pay the taxes on the gains? You can beat these tax-free investments by even conservative stock techniques.

Your side funds will grow at a much faster rate if you can keep from selling off part of the investment to pay your current taxes. This procedure is especially important in the early years when you are trying to build up the value of your investment assets. For example, the income and capital gains from any mutual fund of stocks you are holding will probably be taxed for the year in which these distributions occur. It is often better to let these distributions purchase additional shares in the fund if you are seeking benefits from compounding, and use other cash to cover the yearly taxes.

The profit on stocks that have appreciated in value will not be taxed until sold. You will generally tend to trade less while reaching for higher gains in a taxable portfolio than you would with the pension plan portfolio. In some cases, you will face some mental difficulty in selling certain stocks because you will incur a high tax payment. You could always wait until a change occurs in the taxing of capital gains, but that change may not happen. The reasonable tax rates of the 1986 bill should not inhibit you from taking a large gain at any time. After all, it is always better to pay the taxes on a gain than not to have the gain in the first place. There is no use holding a stock with little dividend return and watch it drop 40% to 60% in value during a pull-back in the market just because you considered the tax consequence. Successful stock investing must let the tax burden play second fiddle.

An advantage of the taxable investment portfolio is that any losses incurred do count against the gains in any securities that are sold in that given year. That fact allows you to rid yourself of some stocks that have performed poorly and to achieve tax benefits on the sale.

CASH HOLDINGS IN YOUR PROGRAM

I have already stressed how important it is for a pension plan to hold an effective percentage of its portfolio in cash. That philosophy also works well for the taxable fund. In fact, if both the pension and personal accounts are stock-oriented, it is advantageous to ballast the cash of one account against the other. That is another reason why I suggest that both the pension and taxable accounts should match well together if both portfolios are invested in stocks. Why not balance one fund against the other to make yourself feel comfortable with your cash position at the extreme ends of any market cycle?

The amount of cash in a personal taxable fund should be at its highest level when the valuation of the stock market is perceived to be near its bottom zone. The economy is generally in not too good a shape at stock market bottoms, and personal cash looks like a desirable commodity to have for a multitude of reasons. Who knows, maybe someone will offer you a delightful condo at the beach for peanuts (translation – small cash outlay).

At times of market bottoms, the stock prices of the smaller companies in the taxable portfolio should also be well-depressed. These stocks tend to stay depressed, on average, for a little time after the economy begins its recovery. So cash in the taxable account usually does not have to be committed quickly at a market bottom. The amount of cash should represent about 50% of the asset base in your portfolio at these times.

How to go about achieving a large cash position in your taxable account at market bottom takes a little more effort on your part. This task is certainly more difficult than what you will experience with your pension portfolio. The whole cash raising process starts at market highs. After some stocks are sold at those times, the cash proceeds are held rather than reinvested. As the market drifts down, further cash is raised, mostly by getting out of the stocks that did not perform too well in the previous economic cycle. This is the time to get rid of these types of stocks, even sometimes at a loss, so that you begin to ready yourself for the next upward move in the market.

The action that you would employ in your taxable account continues to be somewhat opposite to the strategy of your pension portfolio. You should try to hang onto some of those secondary and small cap stocks that showed the most promise in the rise of the market. These stocks will no doubt drop in price during the market decline, but may offer the quickest rise in price on any recovery in the market.

The reverse action should occur in your cash reserve during the times when the stock market valuation is rising to a cycle top. Your personal taxable funds should be at a minimum cash position at this point, possibly only at the 10% to 20% level of the total assets in your account. This is the period of the market when you want the maximum gain out of your stock position, so that the prices of your stocks should be generally left alone to rise to their best levels. The use of the stop-loss order (with stocks listed with the NYSE or ASE) is a good strategy for the protection of some of these gains.

STOCKS CHOSEN FOR TAXABLE ACCOUNT

I believe you should be convinced by now just what a few percent difference in gains can mean for your future investment success. You should set your mind toward earning those extra few percents on your personal funds because of the effect of taxes on the net return of your investments. This quest for higher gains in your personal portfolio steers you toward a diverse group of companies which must be viewed somewhat differently than the stocks recommended for the pension plan portfolio.

The companies chosen for a personal account should be relatively small, with greater potential of growth in their line of business, having little or no dividend pay-out, and usually priced at relatively low levels when first purchased. Many of these companies will have less than 300 million dollars in assets, and will lean toward the high-tech and service industries. Recently, bio-technical and small pharmaceutical companies appear to provide good investment potential.

Your initial portfolio could also consist of at least 50% of the companies from the over-the-counter (O-T-C) market with the remainder coming from the ASE and NYSE. But this is just a suggestion. You might well have over 50% of the companies in your portfolio from the O-T-C group and still be quite comfortable. In fact, some of the companies in the O-T-C market are included in the S&P 500 index group. Small companies which have been around at least ten years and are listed in the Standard & Poor Guide would be good candidates for consideration in a portfolio. In other words, try to stay away from newly-formed companies and so-called penny stocks. However, once some small companies have gotten past the first couple of years of operation, they might offer the greatest opportunity for safe price appreciation in its stock. These stocks could make up about 10% of the total stock value of a portfolio at various points in time.

You probably should consider investing in about 10 to 15 of the small capitalization companies. Since the investment risk is greater with less-established companies, it is prudent to spread your risk over at least this number of stocks. This would indicate that a group of 25 companies should be monitored in about the same manner as the pension program. As your personal assets grow in value in later years, you might decide to increase the number of stocks in both the portfolio and monitor groups. The limiting factor for the actual number of companies you might follow in a taxable program really boils down to the available time and money you have at each stage of your life. You will probably find that a stock program with smaller companies might also take more time than would be the case for the pension plan. One main reason for this is that you have to be more vigilant about any changes that would occur in the financial status of these companies. Secondly, you will find it more difficult to stay with the same smaller companies year after year, especially if you begin to trade for substantial profits. Therefore, be careful you do not dilute your primary effort, that is, to make your tax-deferred pension assets grow at a satisfactory rate.

I hesitated to include this chapter in a book primarily devoted to the investment of stocks for a pension portfolio. But I know there are persons with many more assets in their taxable accounts than in their tax-deferred programs. Some of the ideas of this chapter are directed to them. There is an advantage for using more of a balance between the conservative large company stocks and the smaller cap stocks in their situation. It still comes down to your personal comfort level, just like the investors who might prefer to have a Buy and Hold group of stocks even as they actively trade other stocks within their pension portfolios.

The companies that comprise your monitored list can come from many different sources including advisory letters, broker, television and newspaper analysts, or personal contact with the company's product or service. Financial magazines often show tabulations of interesting secondary or speculative stocks that might supply some names that catch your eye. Once you get the name, some of the pertinent facts you are now familiar with must be researched before you accept the company into your list of possible stock purchases.

The small cap stocks should also be bought near the low price end of the last couple years, but you can be a little flexible and buy in at a higher price for some companies that have what you consider are healthy business signs. These judgement calls occur from time to time, and while mistakes are made, that is part of the learning process dealing with the smaller capitalization companies.

The smaller companies have advantages in that their stock prices are often much lower than that of the large, mature companies. Frequently, you will observe prices much less than $20 per share so you can afford to invest into a greater number of companies during the early years of your portfolio. Since you are seeking greater price gains in these stock positions when compared to the pension portfolio, the greater the number of companies held in your portfolio tends to increase your odds that one or two of them will appreciate in price several fold. Always diversify your purchases into as many industry groups as possible.

The smaller cap stocks can also be purchased by institutions, but to a lesser degree than with the large companies. In most cases, the small company stocks you will review will have less than 10 million shares of common stock outstanding. The fact that institutions are interested in the smaller company is a good sign.

Probably of greater interest is how much of the outstanding stock is owned by insiders of the company. You will have to delve into the company reports, and sometimes the financial company data sheets, in order to obtain this information. A high percent of stock owned by the founders of the company tends to be a good sign for investors.

Another advantage in concentrating smaller cap stocks in your taxable account is that you can balance their business activity against that of the large cap stocks that you should be holding in your pension plan portfolio. Play it safe, and work both sides of the street.

SOME BUY AND SELL STRATEGY

I am much more knowledgeable about the buy and sell strategy for the large company stocks that are gathered in the tax-deferred pension plan. However, you cannot be exposed to the stock market without learning something about how to invest in small capitalization companies. While there have been many successful investors in the small cap stocks, I still consider it difficult to attain success if you do not adhere to certain safeguards in your buy and sell decisions.

The small company stock will be more apt to get involved with a hot tip than the larger mature company. It appears prudent not to jump too fast for a stock purchase that is based on a rumor, especially during the early years as you build up the value of your portfolio. If you do want to take a flyer on a hot tip, do it with only a small portion of your available cash.

You should always remember that most of the new companies that go public will start out with a relatively small number of common shares. This situation will cause a much greater swing in the price of the stock as it trades, in either the up or down direction. That is why you should hesitate taking a position into a small company's stock after it has already had a strong rise in price. There might be a further potential for gain, but one bit of bad news and 30% to 50% of its price could be wiped out in one day.

Investment in the new companies that go public has been a fertile area for some persons. This is especially true when the company is perceived to be in a growing field, or has developed an exciting product or process that has been well publicized.

These new stock issues might come to your attention through your broker. Most of the time when these stocks go public, you might first see a significant rise in their price for a while, and then a decline in price might occur later. If you ever get involved in this type of investing, and I call it a form of speculation, you could buy some of the newly issued stock, take a chance for a fast 30% to 40% rise in price, and then get out with your profit. You might later return to this same stock down the road if you observe its price action for a couple years, and then purchase it at a more reasonable PE ratio within its pricing cycle. Now, I know that this approach will not allow you to brag occasionally at a cocktail party about how you made a killing in the market, but it sure will allow your assets to grow, albeit in a slow manner.

I suggest that you always remain cautious about the speculative low priced stocks. And this caution should extend to some of the older companies which have fallen on hard times or have given into bankruptcy. It will become very easy for you to want to purchase a great number of shares when you see a price, say, below $2 per share. However, if you did buy 2000 shares and the company fails, you have just lost maybe $4,000 of your assets.

You should try to minimize losses in your taxable account of stocks with as much care as you would apply in your pension plan.

Along these same lines, I would caution you to think more in terms of equal amounts of shares for a stock purchase than to equalize the dollar amounts. This procedure may cost you more in brokerage commissions for the low priced stocks, but I believe that you are on safer ground, at least until you become more experienced with the ways of small company investment.

For example, in general, the $2 stock is much more speculative than a $20 stock trading at a reasonable price-earnings ratio. If you bought 200 shares of the $2 stock, you should be mentally prepared to either lose it all or be shooting for maybe a five-fold increase in it's value. Therefore, the 200 shares might produce about $1600 in profit down the road if you are fortunate. On the other hand, the $20 stock is much less apt to turn into a loss. Indeed, the odds should be good for a 40% gain, if you had purchased it according to the concepts in this book. That 40% gain also gives you about $1600 in profit. The amount of profit is the same in either case. Moreover, in the case of the $2 stock, you only had $400 at risk with the 200 shares, as opposed to a potential loss of $4,000 if you had purchased the 2,000 share block. Remember one concept stated earlier – do not be greedy!

One difference between the pension and the personal-taxable stock portfolio is how you handle repeat purchases of a specific stock. While I often like buying more stock of the larger, conservative company at a reduced price, that same strategy is not suggested for the small company. For example, if you bought a stock for $8 per share, and saw it's price drop to $4, I would suggest you resist the temptation to double up on your original purchase.

Conversely, while you would refrain from chasing the large company stock, you could be prone to buy an additional block of shares in a small company if its price rose on some good news. I would still play it somewhat cautious, but if the stock rose in price from, say, $8 to $11 on a good earnings report, another purchase at this higher level appears reasonable. You might be able to ride this stock for an appreciable gain in price, but always remember the technique of the stop-loss order, and where it can be applied, in order to protect your profit.

I believe that in time, you will develop your own common sense rules for investing in the stocks of small companies. Some of these companies will be held for years, while others will be traded often. Let your observations be your guide as you monitor their price trends. You should develop more flexibility in your thinking when it comes to small companies, but I caution you against too much deviation from the basic investment discipline that you developed for your pension plan. The continuous growth of assets in your taxable account, even if it occurs at a slow pace, is synonymous with success for your retirement.

MUTUAL FUNDS FOR THE TAXABLE ACCOUNT

Many of the concepts covered earlier about investments in mutual funds for the pension plan are valid for the taxable account. The use of mutual funds makes it easy to diversity into a large number of small company stocks while you enjoy a greater feeling of safety at the beginning of your taxable program.

This feeling of safety has to come at a price, because the large number of companies held in these small cap funds usually dampens the growth aspect of the individual stocks. Of course, this also works to nullify the loss of a stock. Most of the mutual funds of small growth companies will follow the main trend of the stock market, but at some bias to the large, mature companies. In the first five to ten years of your taxable account, certainly if you are below forty years of age, the more apt you might be to start out with these small company funds.

Most of the larger families of mutual funds have a sufficient selection of funds so that you need not leave the firm to be able to further diversify. However, there is nothing wrong with investing in the funds of several different firms at the same time. Every mutual fund family will have a money market fund along with stock funds. This makes it easy to shift assets from the stock to a cash position. However, some funds may not allow frequent transfers in this manner.

Do not invest any money into mutual funds until you have had a chance to check the record of the fund for the last five years. Review the performances of these funds against other funds that invest in the same type of stocks. Several of the financial magazines rate these funds periodically. Read the prospectus of the fund carefully so you understand what their investing objectives are before you invest any money. And be comfortable with the companies and the industrial groups that make up the portfolio of the fund.

You will want higher growth rates for your personal savings so you might want to check out the size of the fund. On balance, the smaller the size of the fund, the better chance you have for a good return on your investment. However, sometimes you will see the good performance of one year vanish in the next for some of these funds.

CHAPTER 8: STOCK MARKET UPDATE

I have been writing this book for a number of years, but it has been especially interesting to observe my program's success during the last couple of years when certain events have produced significant variations in stock prices. We have experienced a dragged-out recession, a Persian Gulf war, a major drop in interest rates, and new highs in the market averages. And my concepts for the trading of conservative stocks in a pension plan have held up well throughout all these events.

The effect of the above events on stock prices can be seen in a number of charts included in the Appendix. The saying, "a picture is worth a 1000 words," is still pretty true for the purpose of explanation. Even though I'll discuss each figure in terms of how you might have proceeded in your trading program during the changes that occurred, I do not want to infer that the last couple years were so unique that such opportunities will not be seen again.

What I do want to stress is that a countless number of new events in the years ahead will continue to produce an effect on stock prices that, as J.P. Morgan so aptly said, "keep going up and down." At the same time , the concepts that will allow you to trade in these up and down patterns of prices should be considered timeless. Mistakes will be made, of course, and changes are sure to occur, but the marriage of the basic technique of this book to the variations in stock prices should be a lasting one. It is also possible that the DJIA could reach 4000 within the next year or so, or the Dow could drop to the 1500 level. So the marriage can be an exciting one.

Companies will come and go in your portfolio and monitored list of stocks. For example, the monitored list that I am following in February 1992 is shown in Table 8-1 of the Appendix. This can be compared to the list of companies that I followed in June of 1990, shown in Table 5-1.

134

Companies were deleted or added in the period between the 1990 and 1992 lists for various reasons. In the case of Emerson Electric, for example, the stock just gradually drifted up to a higher price level without showing the price action I was seeking. DuPont and Greyhound-Dial stocks were sold out at a profit, and their share prices then kept rising much beyond the trading range I had earmarked for these companies. Certainly that was my mistake in judgment, but that happens, and these premature sales must be accepted as part of the process. At any point in time, these companies could return to the monitor tabulation because I continue to peruse their stock prices, waiting their return to the lower levels of their ranges. General Motors and K-Mart were added to the Table 8-1 list because the price action of the Ford and Sears stocks warranted a double entry into those industry groups. In fact, it can often be satisfactory to own the stock of all four companies at the same time in your portfolio, if the investment timing appears desirable.

I would like to stress again that you are basically recording the price action of the stocks of twenty companies, on a week-to-week basis, from which you make your actual transaction decisions. You should only be invested in a small group of the companies from your monitor list at any one time, even though you actively follow all of the companies. A slow evolution process occurs as new companies rotate into and out of your monitor list. You can consider yourself fairly successful if you are right only 50% of the time in choosing a company that you can use for the trading of its stocks for reasonable profits.

The guidelines discussed earlier in the book simply say that once the stock of a company is purchased, some event will come along to shift its price. Let's see how that scenario might have occurred in the last couple years by the use of the charts shown in the Appendix. These charts use the price variation of selected stocks from the tabulation of Table 8-1. The stock prices are compared to each other as well as to the DJIA of the market for 4 - 14 week periods starting in January 1990. The last set of data concludes in February 1992.

Each of the time periods shown in the charts provide a fascinating look at the pulsations of the stock market. These charts, identified as Figures 8-2 to 8-6, produce a trend equivalent to what your weekly record will show you in tabulation form. I believe that you will find the weekly notation of stock prices to be sufficient for your program, but you may prefer the chart approach.

The next sections will cover some strategy that you might have employed during each of the time periods that are shown in the charts. It is always easy to see what you could have done in hindsight, but this knowledge can be useful to prepare you for next events that shape the direction of the market. This information should supplement and strengthen many of the guidelines and ideas that were contained earlier in the text.

PERIOD - JANUARY TO APRIL 1990

Figure 8-2 shows a 14-week period that produced a range in the DJIA of about 190 points. This size of point spread would be considered a fairly stable trading zone at the high valuation level observed in the Dow. Talk of recession and the memories of the October 1989 break in the market were still pretty fresh in everyone's mind.

Sears went through an up and down swing of about 11% in its price as shown in the top chart. If you look at the Apple and Ford plots, they follow the rise of the Dow average, while the price of the Witco stock stayed flat during the period. The Apple stock went from a low of 32^3/_4$ to a high of 43^1/_4$ for about a 32% gain within an 11 week period. Certainly, this size of gain presents a good chance for a meaningful trading profit.

These normal trading zones of 5% to 10% in the DJIA will occur more often than the periods of strong upward or downward price trends. You might find 2 to 5 of the twenty companies in a monitor list to be potential trade candidates each month, especially during the type of market oscillations seen in Figure 8-2.

In our scenario, your cash reserve would be in a safe zone of about 50% of your portfolio assets because the Dow level is just below its all-time high. Nervousness about the economy would dampen your enthusiasm somewhat. When the DJIA is high, a market decline is prone to be steep, so you would revert to a hedge type of trading posture where smaller gains are earmarked for your transactions. Profits of 10% to 15% that can be obtained in the Sears, Ford, and Apple issues, at any time during this period, are prudent.

PERIOD - JULY TO OCTOBER 1990

The effect of the Iraqi invasion of Kuwait in early August is shown in Figure 8-3. The DJIA was drifting down prior to the actual invasion, as reports of the troop movements were aired, and continued its steady downward path to about 2400 reached on October 12. Overall, the swing in the Dow from the high to low average was about 560 points, or about 3 times the range observed in Figure 8-2. This amounted to about a 19% decline in the DJIA during a 13-week period. Any severe down-turn in the market should drag down most of the stocks and you can see that this occurred with the companies of interest in the charts. Percentage declines in the Sears, Apple, Ford, and Witco stocks were 33%, 31%, 29%, and 39% respectively.

Every significant decline in the stock market tends to follow a different trend path versus time. The October 1987 break of about 500 points in the Dow occurred in one day. Sometimes, the market decline will take a slow meandering trip that might last for many months. What should be uppermost in your mind is the price level of the stocks you are following, rather than how much time is involved in the market decline.

The guidelines of the technique would have had you with about 50% of your portfolio in cash around the middle of July 1990. If you had the benefit of knowing that some of your stocks would drift down about 30% in price within 13 weeks, you no doubt would have raised more cash at the beginning of the decline. But you did not have this knowledge, and it is usually quite difficult for investors to shed stocks at the start of most major declines. I believe that most of us have a natural inclination to not act when the market situation is unclear, especially when there is more cash in your portfolio.

If we assume you did nothing with your portfolio in early August 1990, the market decline would have decreased the value of your stocks. Conversely, the cash reserve in your portfolio would have increased its percentage relative to your stock position. When your cash reserve would have reached the 55% to 60% range of your portfolio value, it would be easy for you to buy some of the declining stocks at prices 15% to 20% below those seen at the end of July 1990. This buying process would continue throughout the downward market trend, in some cases even employing the use of the open buy order.

As the prices of some of your stocks start reaching recent historic lows, or maybe 30% to 35% below their highs of the preceding year, it is conceivable that you would have reduced your cash reserve to about a 20% position of your portfolio. Two reasons would keep you from converting more of your cash into stocks. The market was considered fairly high by historic standards, and the Middle East situation was still in limbo.

The mechanics of the trading technique would not be difficult for you to comprehend. However, the best investment success from its use is still tied to a reasonable understanding of what events are shaping the pattern of the market. Some of these factors were briefly discussed in Chapter 3. If you kept up a little interest on the daily news, you would have found it pretty easy to judge the one key impact on the movements of stocks.

In the case of the Kuwait invasion, the disruption of oil supplies was primarily discussed in the news media. Increased oil cost superimposed on an already weak economy is the stuff of which stock market declines are made. In fact, oil is such an important commodity that the inclusion of an oil company in your portfolio is always a good investment strategy.

Moreover, once the decline was apparent, you would form some judgement of the effect of the oil factor on the four companies you were following as shown in Figure 8-3. This scenario is not an imperative part of the trading technique, but you might as well sharpen your perception as to how events affect the prices of your stocks. It might add to your portfolio results as well as add to your enjoyment when you hit it right. If you do not make the right stock decision based on some event, don't worry. As a practical matter, you will probably find you have not lost much in the overall picture as long as you stick to the basic guidelines of the technique.

Without any benefit of hindsight, you might have made a judgement after the invasion of Kuwait that Ford and Witco would probably be hurt more by an oil supply problem than Sears or Apple. Therefore, these latter stocks would be considered your first purchases on a downward slide in their prices. However, once the stock prices stabilized at bargain levels, the Ford and Witco stocks became interesting because of the potential of their price recovery when the Middle East problem would be solved. (I said when and not if – successful stock investment needs optimism or you will lose many opportunities along the way).

It is difficult to handle the type of market decline seen in Figure 8-3 unless you develop some confidence in the trading technique. Simply stated, it requires you to buy more stocks with available cash while forgetting about the declining value of the prior stock holdings of your portfolio. The original stocks holdings will eventually return to their prior values, but it will be the price appreciation of the new stocks you bought at depressed levels that leads you back to a satisfactory overall growth in your assets.

PERIOD - DECEMBER 1990 TO MARCH 1991

Things did not vary too much in the stock market prior to the start of Desert Storm, but the success of the first few days of the war were clearly seen in Figure 8-4. Apple even moved up about $4 in the preceding week of January 7, for some business reason. The market decline shown in Figure 8-3 is almost a complete reversal to that seen in the rising trend of Figure 8-4. All four stocks participated in the rise of the market during the period of the war.

The market increased about 17% in value during the January 11 to February 15 period as measured by the DJIA. At the same time, the percentage gains in the Sears, Apple, Ford, and Witco stocks were 33%, 23%, 23%, and 22% respectively. Some of the stocks kept rising in price in the aftermath of the war, such as Apple and Ford, while others reflected the still basically soft economy. Some stocks, such as Sears, actually started to retreat somewhat in price. The stock market pretty well reverted to a normal trading pattern until the end of the year.

I guess that if the start of Desert Storm had turned out differently, the chart patterns of Figure 8-4 would also have been different. As it happened, the market took off on an upward trend. If you had purchased stocks during the previous market decline, you would have found yourself about 80% invested in stocks and 20% in cash. Those numbers are not etched in stone, but you certainly would have been on the low cash side in your portfolio.

How fast you raised the cash to stock ratio in your portfolio would have been a personal judgement for you over time. A lot depends on the state of the economy and at what DJIA level the market rise begins. I would personally have been more comfortable in February 1991 with more cash on hand. If that coincides with your thinking, you could have then sold off some of your stock position for 15% to 20% profits in order to quickly get your cash reserve back to at least a 30% level. As your comfort zone improved with a little extra cash, you would slow up your cash raising process somewhat. But you never know when stock prices will stabilize and turn, so you kept taking profits on the upward rise as you prepared to purchase stocks again in the future. Your resting zone would have been around the 50% cash position in your portfolio.

PERIOD - NOVEMBER 1991 TO FEBRUARY 1992

A major drop in the discount rate to $3^1/_2\%$ in the latter part of December 1991 produced a strong rally in the financial markets. The rate cut significantly affected interest rates charged to both business and consumers. This action by the Federal Reserve Board generated some impetus to the economy, which had been floundering since 1990. It is hard to tell how this is all going to play out in the years ahead, but rest assured that the stock market will be an interesting place to be as a participant.

Figure 8-5 shows a graphic picture of what happened to the stock prices of the four companies we are following both before and after the cut in the discount rate. You will note that the stock prices on November 15, 1991 are different from those seen in the March period of Figure 8-4. The Ford stock had drifted down to about a $25 level, Apple stock also declined to $50, while the Sears and Witco stocks were riding a few dollars higher than the prices observed in March 1991.

Further price deterioration in these stocks occurred just prior to the middle of December. The economy was still weak, and auto and house sales were especially poor. The end-of-year selling of stocks for tax purposes was another possible factor for the action of the late November-December market. Since you would have been sitting with a high cash position in early December 1991, you might have considered the purchase of some Ford stock because its price was at a depressed level. The Apple stock might also have been considered because it had been around $66 just a half year earlier. Sears always appeared to be a good buy at $34, as least in recent years, because that is a fair valuation for this conservative stock.

This strategy of putting your cash to work by purchasing depressed stocks is easy to understand but is not always easy to accomplish during periods of economic uncertainty. If you had done nothing and retained your full cash position of approximately 50% in early December, you would still have felt comfortable. But being too comfortable is not going to make your portfolio grow at the levels you will begin to expect.

So as soon as the news of the significant drop in the discount rate came out, you should have been mentally ready to act. Here is where some of your knowledge and confidence combined to help you convert more of your cash into the purchase of stocks. Getting back down to about a 20% to 30% cash position in your portfolio would have been a sound approach at this time. And, as the market continued its climb into January 1992, you should have begun your cash raising process all over again by selling stocks. You knew that you wanted to return to that 50% cash level, but you should have been doing it at a profitable steady pace.

You should also have become aware of the daily price action of your stocks during any rapid change in the market so that you could reach for their best prices. A rapid rise in the market might produce the best stock price near the end of the day, while you might want to take your profits early in the day during a declining market. There is no fixed pattern and certainly not all stocks will react the same way. Sometimes, the patterns even reverse.

For example, a 62 point rise in the DJIA on December 30, 1991 produced little change between the high and low stock prices for LaFarge, McDonalds, and USX-Marathon. However, for the Ford, K-Mart, Sears and Witco companies, the differences between the high and low prices were, $1^1/$_8$, $2^1/$_8$, $1, and $1^1/$_4$ respectively with the highs occurring near the end of the day. The December 30 price pattern for K-Mart showed a $48 high, $45^7/$_8$ low, and a $47^3/$_4$ close. If you had owned K-Mart at $45^7/$_8$, your additional gain for this stock would have been about 4% if you had held off selling during most of the day.

I have included another group of stocks in Figure 8-6 that covers the same period of time as that of Figure 8-5. You can note that K-Mart followed about the same price pattern as Sears after the cut in the discount rate. The LaFarge stock, representing a main core of business in cement and building materials, made a sizable gain over its low price of December 13. If you had earlier purchased the LaFarge stock at below $11 per share, you could have considered some shedding of your position at the $15 level. Is it possible for

LaFarge to reach over $20? Yes, it is possible, but the discipline of this technique requires you to take some profits along the way without trying to predict the maximum prices that might be reached in all your stocks.

Figure 8-6 also shows a downward drift in the stock price of USX-Marathon during the same time that other stocks were rising in price. This stock now becomes a possible candidate for purchase. You have to begin to look for the eventual uptick in energy prices. Before you make a decision for the purchase of any stock during this type of market, make sure other stocks in the same industry group are also riding at the low point of their price range.

I hope some of the trading ideas associated with the charts of this chapter have clarified the earlier concepts. Your enthusiasm and interest will grow with success, and success with this technique will only be achieved with the confidence that you gain over time. If you track the up and down movements of the market so you can take reasonable profits in your stock transactions, it will be easy to prepare for your retirement years.

CHAPTER 9: REFERENCES

You could take the core of the investment ideas contained in this book and begin to trade successfully in stocks without a lot of new information. However, it is wise to continue to observe the flow of new ideas and recommendations for stocks that are continually available to all investors.

Some of these new thoughts will confirm what you feel is right, while others will, no doubt, run counter to your investment philosophy. As long as the bulk of the current information you gather keeps offering different viewpoints than your own, you will probably be on pretty safe investing ground as a contrarian. Just never get so cocky as a contrarian that you begin to believe that every opposite viewpoint for the investment of stocks is wrong.

I have only included a small sampling of the literature and information media that is available. You need only peruse the shelves in a library or bookstore to get a feel for the wealth of investment ideas that exist.

BOOKS ON STOCK INVESTING

I read my first book specifically dealing with the contraian method of investing soon after I started to experiment in the trading of certain stocks within their price patterns. I still remember the excitement I felt because here were some mechanical concepts that confirmed what I had seen to provide some success with stocks.

Even the title of the book, *It Can Be Done - Buy Low, Sell High* (Investors Intelligence, Inc., Larchmont, NY, 1973), states the concept well. The author Lewis H. Kirshner, as a private investor, advanced a number of techniques that go counter to established investing practices. Some of his ideas are different than the path I have chosen, but I believe he did not develop the method specifically for the assets of a pension plan.

Another book by David Dreman, *Contrarian Investment Strategy* (Random House, NY, 1979), lays down the advantages of investing in companies which are out of favor. Mr. Dreman has promoted these ideas over the years with columns in *Forbes Magazine* as well as in other media sources. I have followed his theories with interest and he has been a big influence on some of my thinking.

The presentation of contrarian concepts for all investments can be found in a book by Richard E. Band, *Contrary Investing* (McGraw-Hill, NY, 1985). Mr. Band describes the book as "The Insider's Guide to Buying Low and Selling High," and he presents the case well for the contrarian.

One book that I consider a solid discourse on value stock investing is titled, *The Intelligent Investor* by Benjamin Graham (Harper & Row, NY, 4th Ed, 1973). Mr. Graham taught and wrote early about how you should judge the value of the companies in which you might take a stock position. The concepts of Mr. Graham has gathered many disciples, and I believe many investors follow his fundamental guidelines for stock purchases whether they are aware of it or not.

If you are interested in a treatise on the market indicators used by technicians, a book by Norman G. Fosback called *Stock Market Logic* was published by the Institute For Econometric Research, Inc. in 1976. The Institute is located in Fort Lauderdale, FL and Mr. Fosback is associated with this company.

Another recent book that could prove interesting was written by Peter Lynch and titled, *One Up on Wall Street* (Simon & Schuster, NY, 1989). Mr. Lynch was successful in heading a very large mutual fund, and he describes his philosophy of investing that led to an enviable record.

FINANCIAL PUBLICATIONS

I have liked *Forbes Magazine* over the years for providing a good background of financial articles, viewpoints, and tabulations. *Fortune* and *Money* magazines provide similar worthwhile information. Another publication, *Barron's*, looks like a hybrid between the newspaper and magazine format.

The two daily newspapers that concentrate in financial information are *The Wall Street Journal* and the *Investors Business Daily*. *The New York Times* usually covers the daily stock tables in a comprehensive manner in addition to other financial news. It is in these publications where you would find some of the advertisements for the mutual fund companies.

STOCK MARKET ADVISORY SERVICES

The description of the newsletters that provide stock market insights and recommendations was covered in Chapter 4. These publications are usually issued on a weekly, bi-weekly, or monthly basis. The advisors associated with these newsletters are frequently quoted in various media for their market updates.

A newsletter that offers a digest of investment ideas from many other advisors is the *Dick Davis Digest* (P.O. Box 9547, Fort Lauderdale, FL 33310). This is one way to get acquainted with other advisors by their comments and choice of stock recommendations.

One newsletter I was familiar with for a number of years is *Market Logic*. The publisher now has an assortment of newsletters available to its clients (Institute for Econometric Research, Inc., 3471 N. Federal Highway, Fort Lauderdale, FL 33306).

Another newsletter is distributed by Dr. Martin Zweig, who has developed a pretty fair reputation as a wall street pundit. His publication has 18 issues per year. *The Zweig Forecast*, (P.O. Box 2900, Wantagh, NY, 11793).

Two other advisory services are widely used, both as a data base and to provide an insight on the business outlook for the listed companies of their service. Standard & Poor Corp. and Value Line, Inc. supply updates on their monitored companies about every three months. Samples of their reports are included in the Appendix.

TELEVISION PROGRAMS

I am a frequent viewer of several television sources of financial information. These programs can provide an assortment of current statistics and advisor opinions on a daily basis such as viewed on the CNBC/Financial News Network on cable, or the Nightly Business Report on the public broadcasting system. Another program that I rarely miss is "Wall Street Week with Louis Rukeyser." This weekly sampling of investment opinions by analysts and advisors with good reputations offers ideas about where the market is heading and suggests stocks of interest.

All this advice should not make you enter a zone of confusion. Stick with your disciplined program, by all means, and use this information to either add confidence or provide some wariness to your contrarian thinking.

APPENDIX

COMPANY	CASH DIV. EACH YEAR SINCE	DIV. RATE PER SHARE $	INSTIT. HOLDINGS		FINANCIAL POSITION		
			NO. OF COS	% OF OUTST. SHARE	CASH & EQUIV. MIL. $	CURR. ASSETS MIL. $	CURR. LIAB. MIL. $
ALLIED SIGNAL	1887	1.00	390	57	335	4211	3596
ALCOA	1939	1.78	548	74	601	3731	1867
AMERICAN EXPRESS	1870	1.00	732	64	Equity/share = $14.06		
AT&T	1881	1.32	891	28	1273	23089	18903
BETHLEHEM STEEL	1989	0.40	211	74	107	1027	864
BOEING	1942	1.00	837	48	3465	9538	7116
CATERPILLAR	1914	0.60	464	67	100	5920	4050
CHEVRON	1912	3.30	793	42	1600	9037	8788
COCA-COLA	1893	0.96	832	54	1239	4180	3855
DISNEY (WALT)	1957	0.70	682	41	Equity/share = $26.46		
DUPONT	1904	1.68	808	39	2003	12944	10214
EASTMAN KOD.	1902	2.00	760	54	1064	8815	7079
EXXON	1882	2.68	1003	38	1469	16168	19350
GENERAL ELECTRIC	1899	2.20	1246	52	Equity/share = $13.28		
GENERAL MOTORS	1915	1.60	782	36	Equity/share = $26.16		
GOODYEAR	1937	0.40	299	50	288	3237	2356
IBM	1916	4.84	1254	48	3614	37851	26914
INT'L PAPER	1946	1.68	597	63	341	4058	3288
McDONALD's	1976	0.37	733	60	137	507	1071
MERCK	1935	2.52	1081	56	1598	4386	2726
M.M.M	1916	3.12	860	65	565	5740	3309
MORGAN, J.P.	1892	2.18	687	69	Book Value = $28.51		
PHILLIP MORRIS	1928	2.10	1334	61	128	12622	11020
PROCTER GAMBLE	1891	2.00	769	44	1339	9231	8126
SEARS	1935	2.00	561	64	Equity/share = $35.85		
TEXACO	1903	3.20	907	63	784	6402	6226
UNION CARBIDE	1918	1.00	285	49	132	2371	2335
UNITED TECHNOLOGIES	1936	1.80	527	69	566	9059	6150
WESTINGHOUSE	1935	1.40	568	44	1129	5555	5104
WOOLWORTH	1912	1.08	419	64	68	3328	2496

TABLE 3-1   30 COMPANIES COMPRISING THE DJIA
DATA FROM S&P STOCK GUIDE, YEAR END 1991

TABLE 5-1   MONITORED LIST OF COMPANIES
DATA AS OF DECEMBER 31, 1990 [1]

COMPANY	Stock Symb (2)	Finan. Rank of Com. Shares	Div. Rate Per Share $	INSTIT. HOLDINGS		FINANCIAL POSITION		
				No. Of COs	% of Outst. Share	Cash & Equiv Mil. $	Curr. Assets Mil. $	Curr. Liab. Mil. $
Apple	AAPL	B+	0.48	482	67	1044	2339	887
Baxter Intl.	BAX	A-	0.64	548	54	195	3705	1958
DuPont	DD	A	1.68	756	40	1619	13737	11495
Emerson EL.	EMR	A+	1.32	649	62	163	3517	2536
Ford	F	B+	3.00	750	54	Equity/share = $36.86		
Genl. Cinema	GCN	A	0.48	213	45	1115	1685	564
Greyhound-Dial	G	B+	1.40	181	48	Equity/share = $10.58		
Hershey	HSY	A+	0.90	299	29	24	758	514
James River	JR	A-	0.60	265	78	27	2003	855
LaFarge	LAF	B	0.40	72	15	13	605	293
McDonald's	MCD	A+	0.34	721	54	164	515	1028
Millipore	MIL	A	0.44	207	67	46	396	149
Phillips Pet.	P	B	1.12	451	42	1054	3729	3318
PPG	PPG	A+	1.68	436	46	40	2211	1603
Quaker Oats	OAT	A	1.56	372	46	31	1434	1087
Rohm & Haas	ROH	A-	1.24	194	62	50	1000	535
Sears	S	A-	2.00	573	58	Equity/share = $38.21		
USX	X	B-	1.40	538	61	409	3759	3235
Westinghouse	WX	A+	1.40	686	51	939	5036	4862
Witco	WIT	B+	1.72	128	61	180	659	230

(1) Data taken from Standard & Poor Stock Guide, year end 1990
(2) All stocks listed on NYSE except Apple, which is on O-T-C

TABLE 5-2	COMPARISON OF YEARLY STOCK PRICE CHANGES FOR MONITORED STOCKS [1]							
COMPANY	For Year 1988		For Year 1989		For Year 1990		For Year 1991	
	HI Stock Price	Low Stock Price	HI Stock Price	Low Stock Price	HI Stock Price	Low Stock Price	HI Stock Price	Low Stock Price
Apple Comp.	$47^3/_4$	$35^1/_2$	$50^3/_8$	$32^1/_2$	$47^3/_4$	$24^1/_4$	$73^1/_4$	$40^1/_4$
Baxter Intl.	$26^1/_8$	$16^1/_4$	$25^7/_8$	$17^1/_2$	$29^1/_2$	$20^1/_2$	$40^7/_8$	$25^5/_8$
DuPont	31	$25^1/_4$	$42^1/_8$	$28^3/_4$	$42^3/_8$	$31^3/_8$	50	$32^3/_4$
Emerson El.	36	$27^1/_4$	$39^7/_8$	$29^1/_2$	$44^3/_8$	$30^3/_8$	55	$36^7/_8$
Ford	55	38	$56^5/_8$	$41^3/_8$	$49^1/_8$	25	$37^3/_4$	$23^3/_8$
Genl. Cinema	$25^3/_4$	$15^3/_4$	$28^1/_2$	$23^1/_8$	27	$16^1/_2$	$24^3/_4$	$16^1/_2$
Grey-Dial	$36^7/_8$	$25^3/_8$	$37^3/_4$	$28^3/_4$	$32^1/_4$	19	$46^1/_8$	$24^5/_8$
Hershey	$28^5/_8$	$21^7/_8$	$36^7/_8$	$24^3/_4$	$39^5/_8$	$28^1/_4$	$44^1/_2$	$35^1/_8$
James River	$29^3/_4$	$21^1/_8$	$34^3/_8$	$25^3/_4$	$29^1/_4$	$18^1/_2$	$29^1/_4$	17
Lafarge	$20^3/_8$	$11^3/_4$	$20^1/_2$	$15^1/_2$	$19^5/_8$	$8^1/_2$	$15^1/_2$	10
McDonald's	$25^1/_2$	$20^3/_8$	$34^7/_8$	23	$38^1/_2$	25	$39^7/_8$	$26^1/_8$
Millipore	$41^1/_8$	$32^5/_8$	$37^3/_8$	$25^1/_4$	$37^1/_4$	$24^1/_4$	$47^7/_8$	$29^3/_4$
Phillips Pet.	$22^3/_8$	$12^1/_8$	$30^1/_8$	$19^1/_8$	$31^1/_8$	$22^1/_2$	$29^1/_2$	$21^7/_8$
PPG	$46^7/_8$	$31^1/_4$	46	37	$55^1/_4$	$34^1/_2$	$59^3/_8$	$41^1/_2$
Quaker Oats	$61^1/_2$	$38^1/_2$	$68^7/_8$	$49^5/_8$	$59^1/_2$	41	$75^3/_4$	$47^3/_4$
Rohm& Haas	$37^1/_2$	28	$37^1/_2$	31	37	$24^1/_4$	$48^1/_2$	$32^3/_4$
Sears	46	$32^1/_4$	$48^1/_8$	$36^1/_2$	$41^7/_8$	22	$43^1/_2$	$24^3/_8$
USX	$34^5/_8$	$26^5/_8$	$39^1/_2$	$28^7/_8$	$37^1/_2$	$29^5/_8$	Co. Split [2]	
Westinghouse	$28^{11}/_{16}$	$22^{13}/_{16}$	$38^1/_8$	$25^5/_8$	$39^3/_8$	$24^1/_4$	31	$13^3/_4$
Witco	$38^3/_8$	$30^5/_8$	$45^5/_8$	$34^5/_8$	$39^7/_8$	$21^3/_4$	44	$28^7/_8$

(1) Data obtained from year end - S&P Stock Guides
(2) USX split into two separate companies

TABLE 5-3

Work Sheet for Setting Stock Targets

COMPANY	Average of Low Stock Prices For Two Prior Full Years 1988 1989 $	Col. A Initial Target Price for Purchase $	Col.B Acual Price of Purchase $	Col. C Sell Target of Purchase 30% Above Col. B	Col. D 2nd Buy if price Drops Below Col. B 0.85 Times Col. B	Col. E Sell Target of 2nd Purchase 20% Above Col. D
Ford	40	44	$37^{1}/_{8}$	48	32	
Genl. Cinema	19	21				
GreyHound-Dial	27	28	28	36	24	
James River	23	26	$22^{1}/_{8}$	29	19	
Lafarge	14	15				
Sears	34	$34^{1}/_{2}$	$34^{1}/_{2}$	45	29	
Witco	33	36				

Notes on above example from text: Chapter 5

(1) The average of the full two years were obtained from Table 5-2 for selected companies from the monitor list of Table 5-1.

(2) The actual target prices shown in Col. A were determined by checking the two year average against the current prices of these stocks at the start of program on 7/20/90. The target prices can be slightly above or below the two year average prices. These are judgement calls based on guidelines of text.

(3) Greyhound and Sears stocks were bought at target price in order to start sample program. Ford and James River were later purchased by use of open orders. See text.

(4) Table 5-3 is suggested for a guide during the early period of a program. As a practical matter, it is usually phased out later.

TABLE 5-4

RUNNING RECORD OF SECURITIES AND MARKET VALUES ON A WEEKLY BASIS – 1990

WEEK ENDING	7/20	7/27	8/3	8/10	8/17	8/24
DJIA	2,961	2,899	2,810	2,717	2,645	2,533
S&P 500	362	353	335	336	328	311
NO. OF SHARES HELD	200	200	200	200	300	400
CASH RESERVE	13,700	13,700	13.700	13,700	9,990	7,780
TOTAL VALUE OF PORTFOLIO	19,950	20,025	19,760	19,550	19,300	18,820
CASH % OF PORTFOLIO	68	68	69	70	52	41
APPLE COMP.	41	$41^3/_8$	$41^1/_4$	$38^3/_4$	$36^1/_2$	$35^3/_4$
BAXTER INTL.	$26^5/_8$	$25^5/_8$	25	$24^3/_8$	$23^5/_8$	23
DUPONT	$40^1/_2$	$41^1/_8$	$40^7/_8$	$37^1/_2$	$37^3/_8$	$35^1/_4$
EMERSON EL.	41	$40^1/_8$	$38^3/_8$	$35^5/_8$	$33^5/_8$	$33^1/_2$
FORD	$43^1/_4$	$41^1/_2$	$39^7/_8$	$37^3/_4$	$36^1/_4$ [1]	$34^3/_8$ [1]
GENERAL CINEMA	$20^1/_2$	$20^1/_8$	$19^3/_4$	$19^1/_8$	$18^1/_2$	$17^7/_8$
GREYHOUND-DIAL	28 [1]	$29^1/_2$ [1]	$28^1/_8$ [1]	$27^3/_4$ [1]	28 [1]	$25^7/_8$ [1]
HERSHEY	$38^1/_4$	$39^1/_8$	$36^1/_4$	$37^1/_8$	35	$34^1/_4$
JAMES RIVER	26	$25^1/_2$	23	23	24	$22^1/_8$ [1]
LAFARGE	$16^1/_4$	16	$14^3/_8$	$14^5/_8$	$12^5/_8$	$11^7/_8$
MCDONALD'S	36	$31^3/_4$	$30^1/_4$	$29^7/_8$	$28^1/_4$	$27^3/_8$
MILLIPORE	35	$32^3/_8$	$30^3/_4$	$28^7/_8$	$30^1/_2$	$28^1/_8$
PHILLIPS PET.	$28^3/_8$	$27^7/_8$	$29^1/_8$	$29^1/_2$	$29^3/_8$	$27^1/_2$
PPG	54	$51^1/_8$	50	$49^3/_4$	$46^1/_8$	$44^7/_8$
QUAKER OATS	$47^3/_8$	$47^1/_8$	$45^1/_8$	$44^1/_4$	$44^1/_2$	42
ROHM & HAAS	34	$34^7/_8$	$31^3/_8$	$31^7/_8$	$31^1/_2$	$28^5/_8$
SEARS	$34^1/_2$ [1]	$33^3/_4$	$32^1/_2$ [1]	$30^3/_4$ [1]	$28^7/_8$ [1]	28 [1]
USX	$34^1/_4$	$34^1/_2$	$34^7/_8$	$32^3/_4$	$32^1/_2$	$31^3/_4$
WESTINGHOUSE	$38^1/_4$	$36^1/_2$	$34^1/_4$	$32^1/_4$	$31^3/_8$	30
WITCO	$35^7/_8$	$34^1/_8$	$31^1/_8$	$29^7/_8$	$28^1/_2$	$25^3/_8$

Numbers in parenthesis refer to stock position held.

TABLE 5-5

ACCOUNT:

COMPANY	NO. OF SHARES	BOUGHT		SOLD		NET COST OF PURCHASE	NET PROCEEDS OF SALE	NET PROFIT OR (LOSS)	% PROFIT OR (LOSS)
		DATE	PRICE	DATE	PRICE				
GREYHOUND-DIAL	100	7/20/90	28			2839.20			
SEARS	100	7/20/90	$34\frac{1}{2}$			3498.30			

Note: Companies and Figures Refer to Sample in Chapter 5.

TABLE 5-6

Worksheet for the Recording of Open Orders placed with Broker

OPEN BUY ORDERS

Company	No of Shares Involved	Date of Order	At Stipulated Price	Actual Price if Fulfilled	Date Order Fulfilled	Date Order Cancelled
Ford	100	7/20/90	$37^1/_8$	$37^1/_8$	8/15/90	-
Gen.Cin.	100	7/20/90	$18^1/_8$	-	-	8/16/90
James Riv	100	7/20/90	$22^1/_8$	$22^1/_8$	8/24/90	-
Lafarge	100	7/20/90	$13^1/_8$	-	-	8/16/90
Witco	100	7/20/90	$30^1/_8$	-	-	8/3/90
Gen. Cin.	100	8/16/90	$16^1/_8$			

Open Sell Orders

Company	No. of Shares Involved	Date of Order	At Stipulated Price	Actual Price if Fulfilled	Date Order Fulfilled	Date Order Cancelled
Ford	100	8/15/90	$47^7/_8{}^*$			

* This order is showen for example purposes. In practice, you would normally wait to enter an open sell order for a prior purchase when its price gets within 10% to 15% of target.

Note: See Text For Sample Description in Chapter 5

TABLE 8-1   MONITORED LIST OF COMPANIES
DATA AS OF DECEMBER 31, 1991[1]

COMPANY	Stock Symb (2)	Finan. Rank of Com. Shares	Div. Rate Per Share $	INSTIT. HOLDINGS		FINANCIAL POSITION		
				No. Of COs	% of Outst. Share	Cash & Equiv Mil. $	Curr. Assets Mil. $	Curr. Liab. Mil. $
Apple	AAPL	B+	0.48	496	67	893	2864	1217
Archer-Dan.-Mid	ADM	A+	0.10	545	50	1264	3021	1227
Baxter Intl.	BAX	B+	0.74	661	62	245	3819	2343
Chemed Corp.	CHE	A-	2.00	60	56	135	213	105
Compaq Comp.	CPQ	NR	–	389	47	438	1516	659
Ford Motor	F	B+	1.60	596	51	7332	20586	21528
Gen. Cinema	GCN	A-	0.52	217	48	453	1412	687
Gen. Motors	GM	B	1.60	782	36	Equity/share = $26.16		
James River	JR	B+	0.60	266	77	39	1538	753
K-Mart	KM	A-	1.76	671	75	459	8546	5041
LaFarge	LAF	B	0.30	58	13	24	656	341
McDonald's	MCD	A+	0.37	733	60	137	507	1071
Millipore	MIL	A	0.48	243	75	80	428	198
Pepsico	PEP	A	0.84	918	54	2204	4870	4541
Phillips Pet.	P	B	1.12	477	46	451	2827	2772
PPG	PPG	A+	1.84	441	47	56	2148	1193
Sears, Roebuck	S	B+	2.00	561	64	Equity/share = $35.85		
USX-Marathon[3]	MRO	NR	1.40	514	70	152	2409	2221
Westinghouse	WX	A	1.40	568	44	1129	5555	5104
Witco Corp.	WIT	B+	1.84	146	70	129	574	216

(1) Data taken from Standard & Poor Stock Guide, year end 1991
(2) All stocks listed on NYSE except Apple, which is on O-T-C
(3) Company Spin-off From USX Corporation

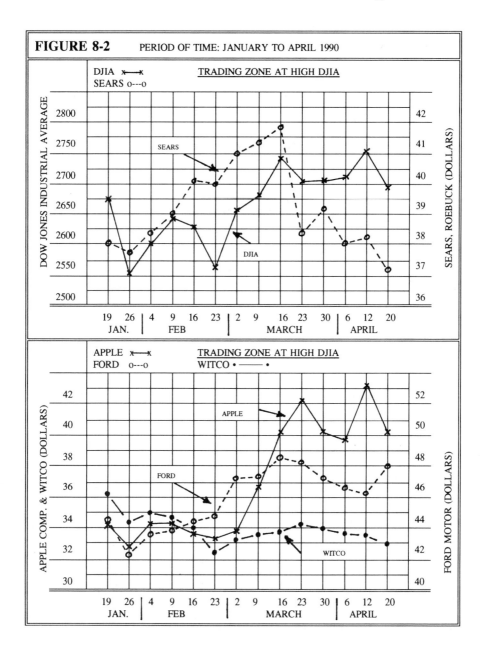

FIGURE 8-2   PERIOD OF TIME: JANUARY TO APRIL 1990

FIGURE 8-3   PERIOD OF TIME: JULY TO OCTOBER 1990

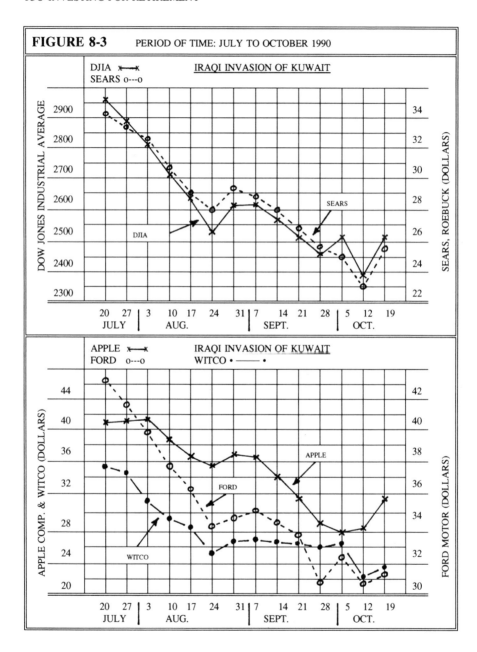

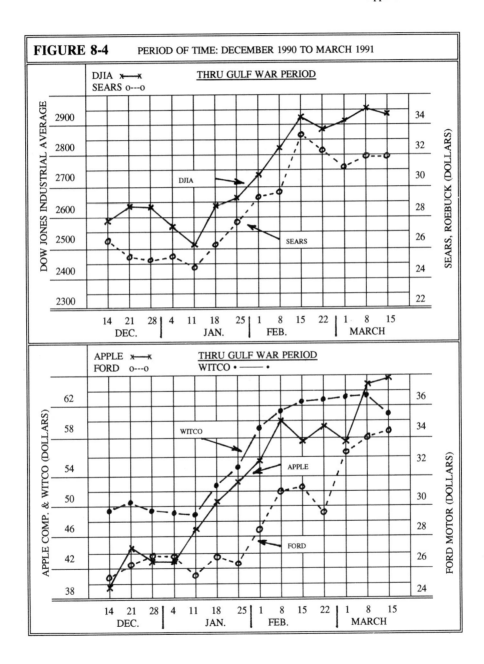

FIGURE 8-4   PERIOD OF TIME: DECEMBER 1990 TO MARCH 1991

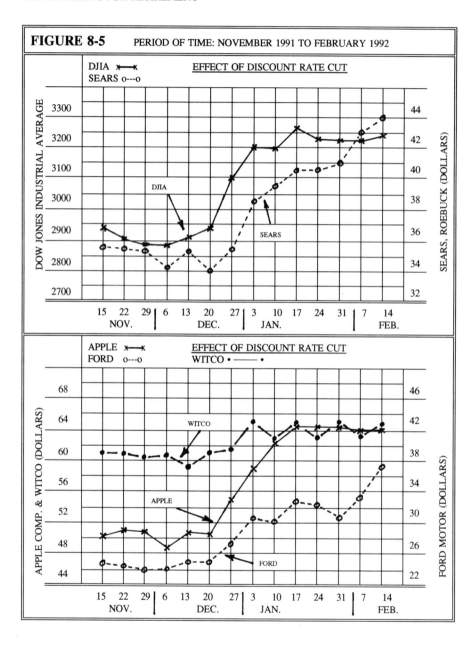

FIGURE 8-5   PERIOD OF TIME: NOVEMBER 1991 TO FEBRUARY 1992

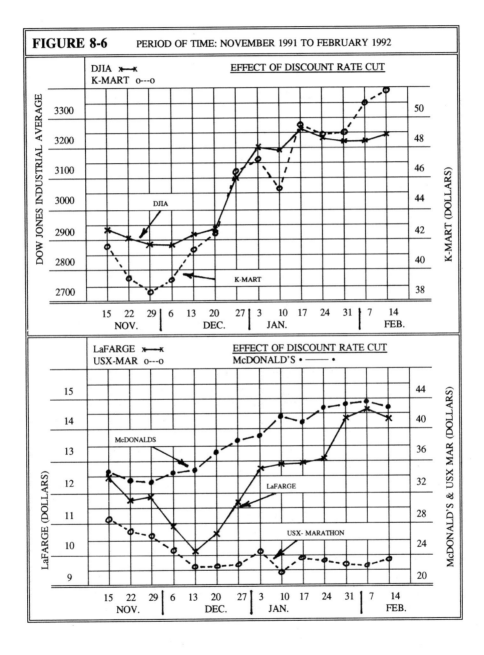

FIGURE 8-6   PERIOD OF TIME: NOVEMBER 1991 TO FEBRUARY 1992

EFFECT OF DISCOUNT RATE CUT

DJIA ✕—✕
K-MART o---o

DOW JONES INDUSTRIAL AVERAGE

K-MART (DOLLARS)

DJIA

K-MART

15 22 29 | 6 13 20 27 | 3 10 17 24 31 | 7 14
NOV.   DEC.   JAN.   FEB.

EFFECT OF DISCOUNT RATE CUT

LaFARGE ✕—✕
USX-MAR o---o   McDONALD'S •———•

LaFARGE (DOLLARS)

McDONALD'S & USX MAR (DOLLARS)

McDONALDS

LaFARGE

USX- MARATHON

15 22 29 | 6 13 20 27 | 3 10 17 24 31 | 7 14
NOV.   DEC.   JAN.   FEB.

Witco Corp.

Sample of S&P Report- Side 1

2495

NYSE Symbol WIT Options on NYSE (Jan-Apr-Jul-Oct) In S&P MidCap 400

Price	Range	P-E Ratio	Dividend	Yield	S&P Ranking	Beta
Dec. 3'91	1991					
38⁷/₈	44-28⁷/₈	14	1.84	4.7%	B+	0.98

Summary

This company produces a wide range of specialty chemical and petroleum products and engineered materials and parts for industrial and consumer use. Recent earnings have been impacted by slow economic growth. Long-term progress is expected to come from internal growth, selective acquisitions in existing business areas, and continued emphasis on cost and manufacturing efficiencies.

Current Outlook

Share earnings for 1992 are projected at about $3.35, up from the $3.10 expected for 1991.

Dividends should remain at $0.46 quarterly.

Sales and earnings in 1992 are expected to benefit from the projected worldwide economic recovery and stronger conditions in the housing, automobile, industrial and durable goods markets. Possible acquisitions in existing business lines would also boost sales. Raw material and crude oil costs are expected to be relatively stable. Profitability should also benefit from continued heavy capital investments (exceeding $75 million in 1991) for plant modernization and expansions as well as for cost reductions.

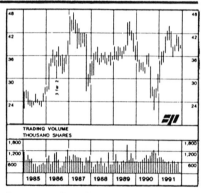

TRADING VOLUME
THOUSAND SHARES

Net Sales (Million $)

Quarter:	1991	1990	1989	1988
Mar.	398	395	400	394
Jun.	421	403	413	405
Sep.	420	419	395	403
Dec.	---	414	380	384
	---	1,631	1,588	1,586

Sales for the nine months ended September 30, 1991, rose 1.8%, year to year, primarily due to higher selling prices in the petroleum segment and acquisitions. In the absence of 1990's nonrecurring gain of $0.19 a share, net income declined 6.0%, to $2.36 a share from $2.46.

Common Share Earnings ($)

Quarter:	1991	1990	1989	1988
Mar.	0.74	0.63	0.86	0.39
Jun.	0.70	0.98	0.97	0.95
Sep.	0.92	0.85	0.86	0.85
Dec.	E0.74	0.49	d1.09	0.86
	E3.10	2.95	1.60	3.05

Important Developments

Oct. '91— WIT said that it was beginning to see a strengthening in the chemical unit, particularly in the U.S. While operations outside the U.S. and in the petroleum business were somewhat flat, WIT was hopeful that fourth-quarter results would show a recovery worldwide. Third-quarter earnings included a $0.02 a share net gain from the sale of the diatomaceous earth business for $10 million.

Mar. '91— WIT said that it achieved the second highest annual earnings in its history in 1990 on record sales, despite a softening world economy and higher, more volatile crude oil prices. The petroleum segment was significantly affected by higher oil costs. Separately, WIT acquired the Duponol surfactant product line from Du Pont for an undisclosed price. During 1990 WIT brought the surfactants and emulsifier businesses of DeSoto, Inc. for $67 million.

Next earnings report expected in early February.

Per Share Data ($)

Yr. End Dec. 31	1990	1989	1988	1987	1986	1985	1984	1983	1982	¹1981
Tangible Bk. Val.	25.11	24.54	24.96	22.11	20.16	18.05	16.27	14.57	13.08	13.10
Cash Flow	4.96	3.46	4.77	4.58	5.18	4.75	4.74	4.19	3.06	3.33
Earnings²	2.95	1.60	3.05	2.72	2.93	2.57	2.85	2.40	1.40	1.84
Dividends	1.720	1.665	1.445	1.200	1.086	0.988	0.960	0.860	0.800	0.755
Payout Ratio	55%	107%	47%	42%	34%	38%	34%	36%	57%	41%
Prices—High	39⁷/₈	45¹/₈	38³/₄	47³/₈	40	27⁷/₈	26³/₈	24⁷/₈	13¹/₈	14
Low	21³/₄	34⁵/₈	30⁵/₈	26⁵/₈	26³/₈	22	18¹/₂	11¹/₂	9¹/₈	10¹/₈
P/E Ratio—	14-7	28-22	13-10	17-10	14-9	11-9	9-6	10-5	9-7	8-5

Data as orig reptd. Adj. for stk. div(s). of 50% Jul. 1986, 50% Jul. 1983. 1. Reflects merger or acquisition. 2. Bef. spec. item(s) of +0.80 in 1988. E-Estimated. d-Deficit.

Standard NYSE Stock Reports
Vol. 58/No. 237/Sec. 28

December 11, 1991

Standard & Poor's Corp.
25 Broadway, NY, NY 10004

Reprinted by Permission by Standard & Poor Corp.

2495   Sample of S&P Report- Side 2

Witco Corporation

Income Data (Million $)

Year Ended Dec. 31	Revs.	Oper. Inc.	% Oper. Inc. of Revs.	Cap. Exp.	Depr.	Int. Exp.	[2]Net Bef. Taxes	Eff. Tax Rate	[3]Net Inc.	% Net Inc. of Revs.	Cash Flow
1990	1,631	149	9.1	90.8	55.3	18.2	106	35.8%	68.0	4.2	123.0
1989	1,588	155	9.7	70.4	52.7	17.6	53	34.5%	35.0	2.2	87.7
1988	1,586	176	11.1	72.1	48.8	18.0	116	38.0%	71.6	4.5	120.4
1987	1,428	153	10.7	69.1	50.0	17.3	100	36.8%	63.3	4.4	113.2
1986	1,355	162	12.0	60.1	50.8	13.6	108	39.8%	*65.2	4.8	115.9
1985	1,449	141	9.7	71.1	48.3	14.0	94	39.4%	56.8	3.9	105.0
1984	1,496	144	9.6	65.7	41.6	16.0	92	32.2%	62.6	4.2	104.1
1983	1,386	133	9.6	44.9	39.0	15.4	90	42.3%	52.0	3.8	90.9
1982	1,305	89	6.8	54.1	35.9	16.1	50	40.5%	*29.8	2.3	95.6
'1981	1,292	102	7.9	55.5	31.8	16.0	68	43.6%	38.6	3.0	70.2

Balance Sheet Data (Million $)

Dec. 31	Cash	Curr. Assets	Curr. Liab.	Ratio	Total Assets	Ret. On Assets	Long Term Debt	Common Equity	Total Inv. Capital	% L T Debt of Cap.	% Ret. on Equity
1990	116	563	204	2.8	1,179	6.0%	230	587	878	26.2	12.0
1989	213	636	180	3.5	1,139	3.1%	236	571	858	27.4	6.1
1988	194	635	196	3.2	1,115	6.6%	241	578	888	27.1	13.1
1987	227	620	203	3.1	1,056	6.7%	243	513	823	29.5	12.9
1986	68	412	165	2.5	820	8.0%	96	464	626	15.3	14.8
1985	83	408	174	2.3	810	7.2%	136	414	604	22.5	14.4
1984	34	367	164	2.2	756	8.4%	143	373	518	27.7	17.6
1983	56	380	177	2.1	733	7.4%	147	334	484	30.4	16.3
1982	49	329	149	2.2	662	4.3%	148	296	447	33.1	10.0
1981	68	396	221	1.8	725	5.6%	150	293	446	33.6	13.6

Data as orig. reptd. 1. Reflects merger or acquisition. 2. Incl. equity in earns. of nonconsol. subs bef. 1990 3. Bef. spec. item(s) in 1988.
4. Reflects accounting change.

Business Summary

Witco Corp. (formerly Witco Chemical Corp.) produces wide range of specialty chemical and petroleum products and engineered materials and parts. Contributions by industry segment:

	Sales	Profits
Petroleum	48%	30%
Chemical	47%	67%
Engineered materials & parts	5%	3%

Foreign operations accounted for 19% of sales in 1990 and 33% of profits.

Petroleum products include white mineral oils, petrolatums, sulfonates, microcrystalline waxes, refrigeration and ink oils, rust preventives, lubricating greases, oils and coatings, naphthenic lubricates, asphalt, rubber chemicals and carbon black produced from refined or semi-refined oils. Crude oil is also refined to produce lubricating oils and sold under the Kendall and Amalie brands, as well as under private labels.

Specialty chemicals include polyester urethane resins and intermediates, surfactants, detergents and cleaners, defoamers, stearates, waxes, fatty acids, glycerines, amines, amides, emusifiers, plastic additives, stabilizers, epoxy plasticizers, anti-oxidants, organic peroxides, metal finishing and treating products, and filtering agents and fillers.

Witco is the leading independent producer of plastic and hard rubber battery containers, covers and parts. It also produces lightweight conveyor belts, molded industrial diaphragms and coated fabrics of plastic and rubber coated cotton, polyester, and nylon.

Dividend Data

Dividends have been paid since 1950. A dividend reinvestment plan is available.

Amt of Divd. $	Date Decl.	Ex-divd. Date	Stock of Record	Payment Date
0.43	Mar. 5	Mar. 7	Mar. 13	Apr. 2'91
0.46	Jun. 4	Jun. 11	Jun. 17	Jul. 3'91
0.46	Sep. 5	Sep. 10	Sep. 16	Oct. 3'91
0.46	Dec. 4	Dec. 10	Dec. 16	Jan. 2'92

Next dividend meeting: early Mar.'92.

Capitalization

Long Term Debt: $223,058,000.

$2.65 Conv. Preferred Stock: 10,348 shs. ($1 par); red. at $66; conv. into 8.4037 com.

Common Stock: 21,776,004 shs. ($5 par).
Institutions hold about 68%.
Shareholders of record: 5,949.

Office—520 Madison Ave, New York, NY 10022-4236. Tel—(212) 605-3800. Chrmn & CEO—W. R. Toller. Pres—D. Andreuzzi VP-Secy—J. Russo. VP-Treas—J. M. Rutledge. VP & Investor Contact—C. R. Soderlind. Dirs—D. Andreuzzi, W. J. Ashe, S. Brinberg, W. G. Burns, S. Friedman, W. R. Grant, H. G. Hohn, W. E. Mahoney, L. J. Polite Jr., D. J. Samuel, R. D. Saunders, L. Scheinbart, H. Sonneborn III, W. R. Toller, B. F. Wesson, W. Wishnick. Transfer Agent & Registrar—First Chicago Trust Co., NYC. Incorporated in Delaware in 1968. Empl—7,365.

Information has been obtained from sources believed to be reliable, but its accuracy and completeness are not guaranteed.   Richard O'Reilly, CFA

Sample of Value Line Report

WITCO CORP., NYSE-WIT | RECENT PRICE **40** | P/E RATIO **12.6** (Trailing: 14.8 / Median: 13.8) | RELATIVE P/E RATIO **0.86** | DIV'D YLD **4.7%** | VALUE LINE **536**

TIMELINESS **3** Average (Relative Price Perform- ance Next 12 Mos.)
SAFETY **2** Average (Scale: 1 Highest to 5 Lowest)
BETA 1.05 (1.00 = Market)

1995-97 PROJECTIONS
	Price	Gain	Ann'l Total Return
High	50	(+25%)	10%
Low	40	(Nil)	5%

Insider Decisions

	J	F	M	A	M	J	J	A	S
to Buy	0	0	1	0	0	0	1	0	0
Options	0	0	0	0	16	3	0	0	
to Sell	0	1	0	1	1	3	2	0	0

Institutional Decisions

	2Q'91	3Q'91	4Q'91
to Buy	36	19	46
to Sell	23	34	24
Hld's(000)	14321	14454	14789

Target Price Range 1995 | 1996 | 1997

Options: NYSE

Shaded areas indicate recessions

1976	1977	1978	1979	1980	1981	1982	1983	1984	1985	1986	1987	1988	1989	1990	1991	1992	1993	© VALUE LINE PUB., INC.	95-97
29.99	32.90	38.50	48.41	58.02	61.64	61.38	63.74	68.31	65.74	60.88	63.89	70.78	70.48	75.35	75.70	79.20	82.75	Sales per sh	94.60
2.00	2.17	2.71	3.20	3.32	3.35	3.10	4.18	4.70	4.91	5.21	5.28	5.37	3.89	5.47	5.85	6.40	6.80	"Cash Flow" per sh	8.35
1.21	1.27	1.72	2.15	2.00	1.84	1.41	2.40	2.81	2.57	2.93	2.91	3.05	1.60	2.76	3.00	3.25	3.50	Earnings per sh(A)	4.25
.40	.44	.51	.60	.69	.76	.80	.86	.96	.99	1.09	1.20	1.45	1.67	1.72	1.81	1.90	1.98	Div'ds Decl'd per sh(B)■	2.20
1.45	1.53	1.64	2.05	2.25	2.65	2.55	2.07	3.00	3.23	2.70	3.09	3.22	3.12	4.20	3.65	3.65	4.55	Cap'l Spending per sh	5.40
8.13	8.95	10.12	11.66	12.96	13.97	13.91	15.37	17.12	18.77	20.86	22.94	25.78	25.34	27.10	28.50	30.05	31.10	Book Value per sh(C)	38.75
18.87	19.22	19.52	19.97	20.26	20.96	21.27	21.74	21.90	22.04	22.26	22.35	22.41	22.53	21.65	21.80	21.90	22.00	Common Shs Outst'g(D)	22.20
6.5	6.7	5.3	5.1	6.3	6.5	7.5	7.8	7.9	9.5	11.7	13.5	11.5	24.0	11.3	12.0	Bold figures are Value Line estimates	Avg Ann'l P/E Ratio	10.5
.83	.88	.72	.74	.84	.79	.83	.66	.74	.77	.79	.91	.95	1.82	.84	.85			Relative P/E Ratio	.90
5.1%	5.2%	5.4%	5.5%	5.5%	6.3%	7.6%	4.6%	4.4%	4.0%	3.2%	3.0%	4.1%	4.3%	5.5%	4.7%			Avg Ann'l Div'd Yield	4.3%

CAPITAL STRUCTURE as of 9/30/91
Total Debt $228.4 mill. Due in 5 Yrs $33.5 mill.
LT Debt $223.1 mill. LT Interest $16.0 mill.
Incl. $150 mill 5½% sub. debs. ('12) cv. into 18.33 shs. at $54.55.
Incl. $10.0 mill. capitalized leases.
(Total interest coverage: 6.0x) (27% of Cap'l)
Leases, Uncapitalized Annual rentals $10.3 mill.
Pension Liability None
Pfd Stock $683,000 Pfd Div'd $27,400
10,348 shs. $2.65 cum. pfd., cv. into 8.4037 com. shs ; redeemable at $66. (less than 1% of Cap'l)
Common Stock 21,776,004 shs. (73% of Cap'l)
(24.6 mill. primary shs.) as of 10/31/91

1305.4	1385.7	1495.8	1448.9	1355.0	1427.7	1585.9	1587.8	1631.5	1650	1725	1820	Sales ($mill)	2100
6.8%	9.6%	9.6%	10.0%	12.0%	10.7%	11.1%	9.7%	9.1%	10.0%	10.5%	10.5%	Operating Margin	11.0%
35.9	30.0	41.6	51.5	50.8	50.0	48.8	52.7	55.3	60.0	65.0	70.0	Depreciation ($mill)	85.0
30.0	52.0	61.3	56.8	65.2	68.1	71.6	35.0	63.2	70.0	75.0	80.0	Net Profit ($mill)	100
40.4%	42.3%	37.4%	39.4%	39.8%	37.0%	38.0%	34.5%	36.0%	34.0%	35.0%	35.0%	Income Tax Rate	35.0%
2.3%	3.8%	4.1%	3.9%	4.8%	4.8%	4.5%	2.2%	3.9%	4.7%	4.3%	4.4%	Net Profit Margin	4.7%
179.7	202.5	202.8	233.5	246.7	417.3	439.3	456.2	359.1	385	415	435	Working Cap'l ($mill)	505
148.9	147.0	143.4	136.0	95.8	242.6	240.7	235.5	230.2	225	225	225	Long-Term Debt ($mill)	225
298.8	336.7	374.8	415.4	465.5	513.6	578.3	571.6	587.5	620	680	700	Net Worth ($mill)	850
8.3%	12.2%	13.2%	11.6%	12.8%	10.1%	9.8%	5.4%	7.7%	9.0%	9.0%	9.5%	% Earned Total Cap'l	10.0%
10.1%	15.4%	16.4%	13.7%	14.0%	13.3%	12.4%	6.1%	10.7%	11.5%	11.5%	11.5%	% Earned Net Worth	12.0%
4.4%	10.0%	10.7%	8.5%	8.8%	8.0%	6.8%	NMF	4.3%	5.5%	6.0%	6.5%	% Retained to Common Eq	6.5%
57%	36%	34%	38%	37%	39%	45%	103%	60%	50%	55%	54%	% All Div'ds to Net Prof	49%

CURRENT POSITION	1989	1990	9/30/91
Cash Assets	213.4	116.4	129.3
Receivables	245.3	261.3	264.2
Inventory (LIFO)	155.0	166.6	159.8
Other	22.2	18.6	21.2
Current Assets	635.9	562.9	574.5
Accts Payable	110.4	139.9	150.0
Debt Due	4.8	5.0	5.3
Other	64.5	58.9	60.5
Current Liab.	179.7	203.8	215.8

ANNUAL RATES	Past 10 Yrs.	Past 5 Yrs.	Est'd '88-'90 to '95-'97
of change (per sh)			
Sales	4.0%	2.0%	4.0%
"Cash Flow"	5.0%	1.5%	7.5%
Earnings	2.5%	-1.0%	8.0%
Dividends	10.5%	11.5%	4.5%
Book Value	8.5%	9.0%	5.5%

Calendar	QUARTERLY SALES ($ mill.)				Full Year
	Mar.31	Jun.30	Sep.30	Dec.31	
1989	399.6	413.4	395.0	379.8	1587.8
1990	395.2	403.3	419.3	413.7	1631.5
1991	398.3	421.3	420.4	410	1650
1992	420	435	445	435	1735
1993	440	455	470	455	1820

Calendar	EARNINGS PER SHARE (A)				Full Year
	Mar.31	Jun.30	Sep.30	Dec.31	
1989	.86	.97	.86	d1.09	1.60
1990	.63	.79	.85	.49	2.76
1991	.74	.70	.92	.64	3.00
1992	.75	.87	.88	.75	3.25
1993	.80	.93	.97	.80	3.50

Calendar	QUARTERLY DIVIDENDS PAID (B)■				Full Year
	Mar.31	Jun.30	Sep.30	Dec.31	
1988	.32	.32	.375	.375	1.39
1989	.375	.375	.43	.43	1.61
1990	.43	.43	.43	.43	1.72
1991	.43	.43	.46	.46	1.78
1992	.46				

BUSINESS: Witco Corporation is a worldwide manufacturer and marketer of a wide range of specialty chemicals, petroleum products, and engineered materials. Chemicals include surfactants, plastics additives, metal soaps, thiochemicals, and filter materials. Petroleum products include Kendall and Amalie motor oils, white oils, petrolatum and waxes. Engineered materials include battery cases and conveyor belts. R&D costs: 1.6% of sales. Has 7,267 employees, 5,949 common shareholders. Insiders control 7.3% of common; INVESCO MIM, 7.7%; Delaware Mgmt. Co., 6.2%. '90 depr. rate: 5.7%. Estimated plant age: 9 years. Chrmn. and C.E.O.: William Toller. Pres.: Denis Andreuzzi. Inc.: DE. Address: 520 Madison Ave., New York, NY 10022. Telephone: 212-605-3800.

Lower oil prices are lifting Witco's profits. The company's petroleum units are paying about $10 a barrel less than they were at this time last year, while generally maintaining selling prices. True, Witco was not able to quickly recover the higher feedstock costs in the fall of 1990 as oil prices rose, but as the worldwide economy remains in the doldrums, we think that oil prices will be fairly stable through 1992. Thus, we look for margins on the petroleum side of Witco to be healthy this year.

Modest economic growth should help the chemicals group. The Allied-Kelite unit, which makes chemicals for metalworking, is an example of a very cyclical business. Any improvement in domestic car sales ought to boost orders for its products. And the Argus division, which makes specialty products used in the manufacture of certain plastics and metals, also would benefit from a better overall economy. All in all, we look for share net to advance about 8% this year to $3.25. Good-yielding, good-quality Witco stock is ranked to perform in line with the market averages over the next six to 12 months.

The company continues to seek acquisitions. Witco has grown in the past by buying other specialty chemical or petroleum businesses that complement its existing portfolio. Now seems to be an opportune time to do some shopping. Although it still has left some of the cash borrowed cheaply in 1987, today's low interest rates make additional debt attractive. However, environmental considerations make small purchases including a plant more difficult now; in some cases, the cost of rectifying a problem could exceed the value of a business. That makes the task of finding suitable candidates a bit more challenging. Absent nondilutive acquisitions, Witco stock offers little appreciation potential over the pull to 1995-97, reflecting the slow-growth characteristics of its businesses.
Michael Schiffman January 3, 1992

Restated Sales (and Operating Margins) by Business Line

	1989	1990	1991	1992
Petroleum	734.6(5.9%)	783.7(4.7%)	770(7.5%)	805(9.9%)
Chemicals	758.8(12.7%)	762.3(10.7%)	800(13.5%)	838(13.5%)
Eng'd Mat'ls	94.4(5.5%)	85.3(4.1%)	93(6.4%)	91(6.4%)
Company Total	1587.8(4.6%)	1631.5(7.5%)	1697(7.5%)	1725(9.1%)
Before corporate expenses, after depreciation

(A) Primary earnings. Excl. nonrecurring gains (losses): '84, 4¢; '87, (19¢); '88, (acct'g change) 81¢; '90, 19¢. Quarterly earnings may not sum to total due to changes in shares outstanding. Next earnings report due late January. (B) Next dividend meeting about March 3. Goes ex about March 10. Dividend payment dates: Jan. 2, April 2, July 3, Oct. 4. ■ Dividend reinvestment plan available. (C) Includes intangibles. In '90: $43.2 million, $2.00/share. (D) In millions, adjusted for stock splits.

Company's Financial Strength	A
Stock's Price Stability	75
Price Growth Persistence	70
Earnings Predictability	45

Reprinted by Permission by Value Line Publishing, Inc.

INDEX